CARL IKEME

WHY NOT ME?

written with
Paul Berry

Six-Four Publications

First published in Great Britain in November, 2019
by Six-Four Publications

Cover Photography: Michelle Maycock

Cover Design: Synaxis Design Consultancy

Photography courtesy of: Sam Bagnall (AMA Sport Photo Agency), Michelle Maycock, Wolves FC, Jackie Cassidy, Sussex Sport Photography, Danny Batth, Paul Berry.

Typesetting: David and Liz Instone

ISBN 978-1-5272-5064-2

Printed and bound by TJ International, Padstow, Cornwall

Contents

Foreword 5
1: A world ripped apart 7
2: The estate's Wembley 9
3: A very deep hole 17
4: Chances with Wolves 22
5: Heading to Christie's 29
6: Making the grade 35
7: Support from Nigeria 41
8: Striving to improve 46
9: A new arrival 52
10: Promoted to the Prem 61
11: "Ride it out, son" 67
12: A Loan Wolf 71
13: Lost vision 78
14: The tactics board 82
15: Acceptance 90
16: Steadying the ship 94
17: "Go well, mate..." 100
18: Wolves roar back 105
19: No quit in me 111
20: Eagles flying high 117
21: "Things are good" 132
22: Back to civilisation 138
23: Hanging up the gloves 146
24: Everything to live for 154
Final thoughts 159

Dedicated to Iris Cassidy and Nnamdi Ikeme

Foreword

Where do I start with you, cousin Carl? To say I'm beyond proud of your achievements would be an understatement! I remember the day you were born and how proud your dad, my Uncle Ike, was. I think he knew someone special had been born. Although you lived in Birmingham and I was in London, we were always connected by way of our parents (your dad and my mum), who were very close. So I was always in the loop about your progress. My mum had a picture of you on the mantle from when you were a few weeks old.

The thing that always struck me about you from when you were young is how quiet and tacit you were but whenever you spoke, it was poignant. You epitomised the saying: 'A man of few words!' I knew you were passionate about football but, with most kids, it's fun until the real work starts. That is when you find out which kids really want to take up the game seriously. And from what Uncle Ike told me about how he was taking you out for goalkeeper training in torrential rain on mire-laden terrain and you still weren't deterred, I then knew that you – my quiet cousin – was deadly serious about this no-nonsense game that is football.

I think it must be an Ikeme thing because that is also my mother's maiden name. We are warriors in spirit, mind and body because while you were treading the football fields, I was treading boards in theatre, relentlessly pursuing my acting career. And, thanks be to God, we both proved to be good, as well as successful, in our chosen art forms.

When you signed for Wolverhampton Wanderers, I was so happy for you because I knew how hard you worked to get your spot in the big leagues and football is hard enough as it is. Mind you, in saying that, you're an Ikeme, so of course you were going to achieve your goals (pun intended lol!). Watching you on TV, you seemed so much bigger than the other players and when you challenged for a ball, you looked powerful and imperious. You had this wonderful presence but at the same time I felt so protective of you. I didn't want anyone hurting my cousin.

It also felt strange because I was naturally torn in allegiance if your team played against Spurs. I am a fan of theirs, so I always hoped those games would end in draws. When I learned you were selected for the Nigerian international team, I was so imbued with pride. I couldn't stop telling anybody, whether they wanted to hear or not: "My cousin plays for Nigeria!" My kids, your nieces and nephews, walked with an extra pep in their step. It truly was a special moment.

When Uncle Ike called to give me the heart-breaking news that you had been diagnosed with leukaemia, it absolutely knocked the stuffing out of me. For a time, I refused to believe that God could allow such tragedy but after wiping my tears and reflecting, I realised that I/we all had to remain strong for you and make sure you got through this ordeal. To touch on what I said earlier, 'Ikeme Warrior blood' runs through our veins, so I never doubted that you would fight and kick the s**t out of this cursed disease. You have shown so much character, guts and bravery and, through that, my pride, respect and love for you has increased.

Although I really wanted you to play on for Wolves and Nigeria, I have always said that you can never walk in another man's shoes and you have to respect their decision. What you achieved in football, some people can only wish for, so in my opinion you retired from the game while on top and, looking back upon it now, you made the right decision.

I really want you to know that our many reflective, inspiring talks about life, the future, family and ambition are confabs that always left me feeling motivated and galvanised to do more in my career and I thank you for that.

God bless you cousin, I love you dearly. We are all so proud of you and your great acheivements and what's so exciting is that there is still more to come.

Your cousin, Charles 'Chucky' Venn

Igbo Kwenu!!! x

1

A world ripped apart

I was in Homebase when I took the call. Buying paint. We were doing a bit of work on the house so I had popped to Sutton Coldfield for supplies. I was away from Wolves training at the time as I had been undergoing tests, but I didn't think it was anything to get too worried about.

I'd been to see a haematologist and had blood tests and a CT scan, but the scan had come back clear. I was thinking I had probably picked up one of those strange viral infections that I had seen affect other players; that I wouldn't be able to train for a few weeks while it worked its way out of my system, and then I'd be able to get back on it, all systems go. To be honest, I was more disappointed that I was going to miss the start of the season.

We were at the start of July, with a new head coach in charge at Wolves, and he was going to start with a new first-choice goalkeeper, leaving me to play catch-up. That is never ideal for a footballer, especially a goalkeeper, when you are fighting for only one position. Then came the call.

It was Wolves' club doctor, Matt Perry. He is brilliant, I had known him for years, and, for us at Wolves, as with his patients when he was a GP, I'm sure, there was complete trust and confidence in him. I have only recently thought about how difficult it might have been for him to make that call. I had known him so long, 15 years or so, and he would have understood only too well the consequences of what he was about to tell me.

When I answered,I just assumed it was going to be another of the regular updates he had been giving me while I went through the series of tests. I walked outside so I could hear him properly, and went over to sit in my car. The Doc started talking, but he had a different tone to normal, quite quiet and sombre. He started talking about Stan Petrov and Geoff Thomas, both of whom had battled with leukaemia, and, slowly but surely, I started to understand where he was going. He told me it was going to be a very tough year for me and for my family.

I can't remember much else, but he must have made himself clear because when we finished the conversation, I knew exactly what was happening. And exactly what was to come. Then I just started crying. Sat in my car on Homebase car park, face flooded with tears. I HAD CANCER.

Straightaway, I was just thinking, or at least trying to think, about what it all meant. To be honest, I don't know what I was thinking. Everything was all messed up. How was my partner Saba going to cope with such devastating news? She was heavily pregnant with our second child. Was I going to be around to see my daughter Mila, so young and innocent, grow up? How was I going to tell my mum this dreadful news? My dad? What would I say?

It was so difficult trying to take in all the information when, in the space of a few minutes, my whole world had been ripped apart. All the emotions came flooding in and everything was flying around in my mind and it just felt impossible to make any sense of it. I guess the best summary is that it was difficult to escape from the thought that the news I had just been given was the equivalent of a death sentence. So yes, that was the main thing I was thinking.

That Wednesday afternoon in the height of summer, sat in my car outside Homebase in Sutton Coldfield, I thought I was going to die.

2

The estate's Wembley

When your world is suddenly turned upside down, and you are faced with real questions about what may happen in the future, it is only natural to start thinking back over your life. Thinking about what you have achieved, everything you have been through, and all the family and friends who have been with you along the way.

For me, growing up was sometimes tough. We lived in a couple of fairly basic flats during my childhood and didn't have a great deal when it came to luxuries or anything beyond what we needed to live on, but I am certainly not complaining. I didn't know anything different and most of the friends I played with were in the same situation. We had a roof over our heads and I had a lot of friends to pass the time of day with – and of course, play football with.

Having been born at the Good Hope Hospital in Sutton Coldfield, I was brought up initially at the Barrie Jackson Flats in Aston, which was my Grandad Nnamdi's place, with Mum and Dad. After a couple of months, we moved to a flat in Stone in Staffordshire, which was the only decent place Mum and Dad could find. We were there for a couple of years and then returned to Castle Bromwich, where I would eventually go to Castle Bromwich Junior School and Park Hall Academy.

Growing up, I thought a lot about football, and Dad tells me that as soon as I started walking, I was trying to kick a ball. He was always a big football fan, but when it came to playing, tennis was more his sport – he is a very good tennis player. For me, I just loved playing outside and getting dirty, and that is why I ended up in goal, being able to dive about. I would end up with damp clothes, and layers of thick mud all over me, and still vividly remember my Mum telling me to take off all the dirty clothes before going back into the flat so I didn't trample that mud everywhere. So, yes, like many kids, I was mad on football. Outside the flats where I grew up, there was an open space and a grass verge. That was what we called our Wembley. It was a small and flat area surrounded by grass levels which were higher, so it felt like a bit of a stadium. It was very small, but as young lads just enjoying being outside and playing football, it seemed a lot bigger at the time.

Mum's washing line was by a tree and, if there weren't any clothes on it, we would put that down and use it as a post. Sometimes we'd carry on even when there was washing out. It's fair to say Mum was never too happy with us on those days.

We'd spend so many happy hours playing on Wembley – headers and volleys, tracking, British Bulldog. I had a really vivid imagination, so I'd be a goalkeeper flinging myself all over the place and impersonating my heroes. I'd be telling my friends I was Peter Schmeichel as I made one save, then Gianluca Pagliuca – he was a good one because he had a bit of flair when he was diving. I'd never just catch the ball easily when I was Pagliuca. I'd be diving around, making saves for the cameras, you know how it is.

While I enjoyed playing in goal, I didn't mind going outfield either, where, once again, I'd use my imagination and pretend to be someone famous. Maybe Ronaldo, the Brazilian striker version, or Jay Jay Okocha, Nigerian of course! I would try and copy the players of the day that I had seen on TV doing certain tricks or producing pieces of skill. To me, it wasn't a patch of grass outside some flats in Castle Bromwich, it was a huge match on the world stage in a sold-out stadium with my mind imagining all the tense emotions of the game. One day I might be playing in an FA Cup Final, the next would be a World Cup. It might have been a bit of fun but I really think the imagination I had helped me later in my career. I always imagined playing football, visualised what could happen, and that just honed and developed my love of the game.

Looking back, I had probably already decided when I was six or seven what I wanted to do. I wanted to be a footballer. Who doesn't at that age? Of course I didn't know then that I would go on to play professionally and have a career but I would often be visualising that from when I was very young. I loved playing football.

It took me a fair bit of time to get some decent boots, though. We were never what I'd describe as poor, but Mum and Dad had to be careful with money and would never splash out by spending over the odds for anything. They knew the value of money, so the Christmas presents would be bought on credit cards, on the 'never never'. Money was very tight, and Mum tells me that when she once decided to take a bit of a gamble and put the grand total of a pound on a horse which won at 8/1, her treat was to buy a mixed kebab and a bottle of Exhibition cider. Proper pushing the boat out! There were certainly never any foreign holidays, but, when I was seven, my Nan Iris moved to Devon. That meant we would often go and stay with her in the school holidays, and that was something I always really enjoyed. I loved spending time with my Nan, playing on the arcades and standing by her as she played the fruit machines.

Back to the football boots.....my first ones were a pair of Patricks, and I looked after them with great care and attention. It's safe to say they weren't what I would have chosen if money had been no object but I was just so happy to have some of my own. Two or three years later, I had a pair of Puma Kings, which were 'the' boots of that time. That still rates as one of my favourite Christmas presents. Puma Kings – yes, I'll take those. Now we were in business!

It was a similar story when it came to kits, and, while Aston Villa was my team as a kid, we didn't really have the money for a nice, expensive replica kit. So it was that the first kit I had was a Heart of Midlothian one! I can't remember if Mum or Nan bought it me but it was something they had seen down the market and thought 'it's claret, that's the same colour, so that'll do!' I eventually got a proper Villa one. I was just mad keen to get my hands on anything to do with football. We didn't have the money for me to have a Subbuteo set either, so I made my own. I had felt tip pens, where I would take the lids off and use one as a football and the pens would play against each other. I would always pretend that I was one of the players, heavily involved in the game.

With Villa as my team, it was handy that when my Dad came over from Nigeria, he lived in Aston with my grandad, who was just ten minutes away from Villa Park. I used to love going to see Grandad on a Saturday afternoon. He'd sometimes be watching the horse racing on the television and then we'd be watching all the football scores coming in on Teletext. I have such fond memories of those Saturdays with him. We didn't often go to games but I remember getting along to one or two as a kid. One memory is of going with Dad, when the Holte End was still all-standing. I recall him pouring a load of whisky into a coke bottle, then giving it to me to carry through the turnstiles. The stewards would never search a young kid and he took it back off me once we were inside.

I loved the atmosphere of the match and standing on the terraces. It was my first taste of the magic of football, and provided more motivation for me to one day go on and play at Villa Park myself. I was seven or eight but a few years later I would go on to play for Villa's Academy which meant I got a free ticket for games. Happy days!

Away from football there were a few mad things that happened around our estate growing up, although to us, at the time, they became seen as normal. I can vividly remember things that were going on, even if I didn't completely understand them. There were alcoholics around the place, and a lot of drugs, violence and crime, but it wasn't something that really bothered me or frightened me. I remember there was a lady in our block of flats who my Mum knew well who was a severe drinker, and because of that she had her children taken away from her. We all thought she had gone away somewhere for a week one Christmas, but it turned out she had passed away, and her body was still there, in her apartment.

People on the estate had their problems, and there was always something going on, but I would never say it was anything that I found difficult to handle.When you haven't got much you don't really know any different, and I was never massively into all the material things in life, and, to be honest, never really have been since. To me, our life, and what we had, was fine. It was the same for everyone on the estate, and I didn't realise that there was this big wide world out there where people had nice houses and cars!

My motivation as I was growing up was more about doing well and looking forward to getting out and doing the very best I could for my family to improve their lives if I could. The environment definitely shapes you, but my love of football gave me a different path to take and a different focus from a very young age. At maybe 13 or 14, a lot of my friends were drinking, smoking, dabbling in drugs.I remember one of them overdosed at the age of 14,fortunately he lived to tell the tale. My love for football and ambitions to become a footballer kept me away from all that, and my Dad was also very well known around the community and very well respected. If anyone had seen me drunk, they would have told him, and then he would have found me and beaten my backside! He knew a lot of people, pretty much everyone in fact, and his friends would always see me knocking about. So if I ever got up to no good, make no mistake he would find out, and, again make no mistake, he would have whooped me!

It is funny now, because my Dad in particular was very strict on me, but if he sees me disciplining my own daughter Mila and giving her a little telling-off, he's like: 'Come on Carl, you can't do that!' The tables have turned. So while I tried to stay out of trouble because I wanted to focus on football, I also stayed out of trouble out of respect for my Dad. That extended into the community as well, because people could see how much I enjoyed football, and realised that I was really trying to give it a go. It might have been a rough and tough place to live from time to time, but everyone looked out for each other, and when they could see someone had a chance of achieving something in their life, they would support them. I think people around the estate knew I had a chance, and that meant everyone would be keeping an eye on me, looking after me, and making sure I made the most of my potential.

Even the 'bad boys' from the local area, the older kids, they would be thinking that I needed to keep away from anything that could get me into trouble or would risk losing the opportunity that I had. There was that togetherness in the community, so even the more dubious characters would see I had the chance to do something with my life and would be getting behind me. Even so, it was still a tough area to grow up in, and a lot of people would just spend the evenings walking from pub to pub.

Our parents would always know where we were, and who we were with. We would walk around the streets and all the adults would recognise us. Now and again they would say, "You're Ike's son", a gentle reminder that they had their eye on me. I would also stick out like a sore thumb because I was so tall. But as I say, I never really wanted to go down that route of getting into trouble, and it never really looked like it was going to happen. Although, even if I didn't get involved in drinking or drugs, maybe there was the odd time when I would end up doing some of the stupid stuff that all kids do.

Being a general nuisance around the area was something I was definitely game for. Trying to get chased by the Police was one of our specialities, and, the advantage of being big and tall was that I was quicker than everyone else, so would always get away. It was just pranks, messing about and stuff, and I remember we'd call the Police and tell them that there were kids loitering around by the shops. We'd be bored, and it would just be to try and get chased and generate a bit of excitement in our otherwise fairly routine lives. So I was game for the mischief, and there were also always scraps going on, but by and large I never got involved in any of that either.

Of course I could look after myself, and I definitely knew how to look after myself, but I wasn't a fighter or an aggressive person. There is nothing I hate more than a bully, but on our estate you had to be able to protect yourself when you needed to. I got on with everyone, even the older kids, and so even when there were problems people tended to leave me alone, particularly for those reasons that they knew I had a chance of getting out and making something of myself.

Sometimes the kids from Castle Vale down the road would come over and try and cause some grief, and we were cheeky little bastards, so we would give them a bit of verbal. They were older than us, and on one occasion I remember they had stolen a car, and they nearly ran my friend over – he had to jump over the bonnet otherwise he would have been. After a while a few of the other lads from the Spitfire pub had noticed that these lads kept coming back to our area, and so they were prepared, with bricks at the ready. I still remember one of the lads hit the driver's window with a knuckle duster, trying to get through it. The 'outsiders' soon disappeared back to Castle Vale, and it's probably no surprise that we didn't see them again after that.

So while we were a bit naughty and got up to mischief, I wouldn't say there was ever anything too sinister. It was just to try and pass the time, and generate some excitement, and the more serious stuff like drink and drugs were never for me. I knew too that I had to be careful, because my Mum and Dad were quite strict. But like any kid, I had my moments, and I remember once Mum put a load of washing up liquid into my mouth because I had sworn. My dad could also have a bit of a short temper, although he has certainly mellowed since then. He went through a tough upbringing in Nigeria and ended up in trouble from time to time, and I probably took a few whacks from him while I was growing up, which no doubt I deserved. That used to be a part of parenting, and it never did me any harm.

I have huge respect and appreciation for what my Mum and Dad have done for me, and still do. They actually split up when I was about 12. They broke up a fair few times when I was growing up but would always get back together. Until the last time, that is. It's never nice when your parents split up but it was probably something of a relief in the end, and I know Mum and Dad think they should have done it a few years earlier. There was a lot of arguing at the time, a fair bit of drinking, and sometimes it escalated into violence. There was a lot to deal with in those days, including racism.

It was a different world back then, and, for a white lady like my Mum, going out with a black man just wasn't seen as the right and proper thing to do. It even took my Mum six months to tell her dad that she was going out with him. From the start, it kind of went against the ethics of everything, going out with someone of a different colour. My mum wouldn't walk down the street with my dad, she would make him walk behind her. She was embarrassed, not by him or because she was going out with him, but about the reaction and attention that it might cause. There were very few black people in the area in any case, and so the curtains were twitching when they were walking down the road, and again after I came along, particularly in Stone.

Mum has also told me about one of her first dates with Dad, at the Monte Carlo Club on the Soho Road. She says Lenny Henry would describe it as the sort of establishment where they would ask you on your way in if you had any offensive weapons – and, if you said 'no', they would advise you to find one!

When we moved to Stone not long after I was born, Dad wasn't completely up for the idea. It was 30 miles from where he was happily settled and a nice area. The only problem was that there was a fair bit of racism there, but Dad was never shy about sticking up for himself. There were only two black people in the village, and the guy in the flat downstairs used to give Dad grief. He had an Alsation which he tried to scare people with, and one day he pulled a screwdriver on my dad, and called him a black bastard, so he promptly whacked him!

It wasn't just in Stone that racism reared its head and a few things happened once we were back in Birmingham as well. One New Year's Eve, my Dad was jumped by a load of youths in Sutton Coldfield who were giving him racial abuse, and my Mum's mate was stabbed with a screwdriver and ended up in hospital. Despite being outnumbered, Dad once again gave as good as he got and the Police then arrived to sort things out.

Obviously, a lot of this racism took place before I came along or was very young, including when I was a baby. Once, when I was only two and we were back in Birmingham, a group of three Irishmen on the bus from Four Oaks to Sutton Coldfield were calling me and Mum horrible names. They were calling me a nigger and mum a nigger-lover, and saying how much they hated black people. Mum told the bus driver, who kicked the men off. She was tough but I think incidents like that, when the abuse was directed towards her son, affected her far more. There was another time when someone saw me in my pram, dressed in shorts, and commented what a nice tan that I'd got. My mum told them I was the same colour in the winter as well. It didn't affect me massively, as having a white mum and a black dad was just normal, just like it was to be living in a flat without a car or any real luxuries. I didn't know anything different. They were just my mum and dad.

We had moved back from Stone when I was two because my grandads were ill and in and out of hospital and my nan was the best babysitter. It was far easier this way. But being in Birmingham caused problems as Mum was working more at the chip shop, earning more and Dad was able to spend and drink more.

There were plenty of arguments until the last one, around the time of Dad's 30th birthday. This one finally proved the end, which was probably a relief, not just for me but for Mum and Dad too.It probably took a bit of getting used to but, after a while, they started getting on really well and became pretty much best mates. Once everything calmed down and the tension disappeared, we became more of a family despite Mum and Dad being apart.

They remained good to me even after the break-up. They have never moved far from each other and now live in the same road. Both found new partners and have had daughters from those relationships, which has given me two siblings, Taylor on Mum's side and Tia on Dad's. To me, they are sisters, not half-sisters or step-sisters, and we are all very close. When it comes to family functions, everyone turns up and gets on, which some people find a bit strange.

When we went to Christie's Hospital during my treatment, there was a lady Nigerian doctor. Mum was with Tia one day and the doctor said: "You're not as tall as your mum, are you?" We didn't say anything, as sometimes it becomes more complicated when you try to explain! Looking back, when I was younger, Mum and Dad were in a cycle which would have hurt all of us more and more had it carried on and spiralled into something which potentially could have been even more serious. I think everyone was on tenterhooks all the time, walking on eggshells, wondering when and where it was all going to kick off again.

After the break-up, Mum and Dad were able to move on and get on with their lives while keeping things normal for me. In those days we didn't have a great deal, but we never went without and I can look back on my childhood with a lot of happiness and so many good memories. They were tough days but they were good days and hopefully I have come out of it and gone on to make my mum and dad proud. Our close relationship meant that when I was struggling and going through everything I have had to go through in the last couple of years, they were both there for me. I was able to see the very best of them and get the very best care when I needed it most.

3

A very deep hole

As I sat in my car at Homebase, it was my family who I immediately started to think about. There was no easy way I could tell them the news that I had just received a phone call to say I had blood cancer. What was making it even more difficult was that there hadn't really been a huge amount of concern at our end and only Saba had known I was even going for tests. I wouldn't even say I had felt particularly unwell.

I had finished 2016/17 with a hamstring injury and my last two games were big wins at Brentford and Fulham which gave us breathing space in getting away from trouble near the foot of the Championship. The lads went on and made sure we secured our status in the division and I was feeling highly optimistic about the future once I could get fit again. I got on really well with Paul Lambert, felt I was still in very good form, and was looking forward to what he might do with the squad. I was having treatment for the last few weeks of the season and then grabbed a week's holiday in Spain with Saba, by now heavily pregnant, Mila, my friend Adam and his partner Michelle and their two children. It was a good break, but Wolves goalkeeping coach Pat Mountain called while I was there to say Paul had left. I have to say that deflated and disappointed me. There had been a couple of difficult years at the club and, in Paul, I felt we had someone who had steadied the ship and had the potential to get us firing again. For me, it was bad news that we were going into the season with a new manager and some uncertainty. I had no idea then of the impact Nuno and his staff would have and the investment the club was going to make during the summer.

Away from that, everything was normal and I came back from holiday ready to work with the Wolves physios. As the hamstring got better, I spent a lot of time with our Wolves keeper Matt Murray, doing additional stuff in the gym. I say I felt fit and normal....looking back, there was probably something missing, something I couldn't put my finger on. I didn't think it was anything too serious, maybe it was down to fitness through not having trained properly for a long time or the disappointment that Paul Lambert had gone.

Maybe it was a mixture of everything but I didn't feel quite 'at it'. I had worked under a few managers in a short space of time and don't know if my mind was a bit affected. I felt okay but maybe just not at the level I wanted to be at, certainly for coming back and trying to impress a new head coach and keeper coach. Still, when I reported for pre-season, I met Nuno and Rui Barbosa for the first time and set about getting down to work. It was then that I started getting a few headaches while training. Again, I didn't worry too much. I'm a fairly big lad and just put it down to returning to training after so long and hitting the floor again with a thump while making saves; in other words, my head rattling as I landed, something that goes with the territory as a goalkeeper.

Maybe there was also a bit of dehydration. It was all a little bit strange but still I wasn't overly concerned. And yet, I did start to develop this feeling in my stomach which I still can't properly describe. Even when I talk to the doctors, they don't really know what it was, as it wasn't any sort of marker or side effect for leukaemia. The only way I can describe it is that I had something living inside me. I remember being in bed some nights and having a feeling of something swimming inside me.I had been for a blood test which revealed that my platelets were low but that wasn't necessarily a problem because they were often a bit low. So still it was a case of perhaps thinking it was a viral infection – I had never really been ill before and, when I was, it was usually clear what the problem was.

Then, the one day, we did a tough session on the grass and I went straight to the gym afterwards. That's me – always wanting to do extra and keep my gym time up! When I went back into the dressing room to go to the toilet, my nose started bleeding. I never have nose bleeds, so this was starting to get strange. For some reason, and I still don't know why, I went and told the club doctor, Matt Perry. Normally, I wouldn't tell the Doc stuff because, as soon as you did, he would probably keep you out of training. And I never wanted to miss training. Sure enough, he told me we would need to keep an eye on it and we would have to pay a visit to the haematologist as soon as it was possible.

Was I becoming worried? A little. I felt there was something going on, but still thought it wouldn't be serious. All players will tell you it is very rare that you feel right all the time and you become used to getting on with things, giving it your best and ignoring health or fitness problems. I thought I might need some antibiotics and it would all clear up. The Doc, the consummate professional, came with me to Little Aston Hospital and I had some blood tests. The haematologist was Manos Nikolousis, who asking a lot of questions. Had I been ill? Suffering from a virus? An infection? Could I feel swelling round my neck?

I remember him saying he was going to check for lymphoma, leukaemia, HIV. He reeled off a whole load of diseases that I was going to be tested for. Let's face it, when you go for any blood test, there is always that feeling of concern about what it might show, so hearing those diseases mentioned wasn't exactly putting me at ease. While we were waiting for the results, I was kept out of training because there was the worry that, if I did take a whack, my blood might not be able to clot properly. I also remember having these marks on my arm and around my shoulder; not so much bruises, but red dots.

I know now it signalled that my platelets were low, but I recall looking at it and thinking I hadn't been hit there or anything. There weren't a load of the spots, but just enough to notice. It wasn't something I had mentioned to anyone previously and still I didn't feel ill or unable to carry on with normal day-to-day life. At the same time, I went in for a CT scan but the Doc phoned me after that to say it had come back fine, so there was some relief there. My over-riding thought was still that disappointment that I was going to miss the start of the season. But on I went, just living normally, and going off to Homebase that Wednesday afternoon. Then came the phone call.

The worst feelings were going through my mind as I sat in the car in tears, not really knowing what to do next or how I was going to tell anyone. I couldn't even tell Saba. She tells me I phoned her a few times and put the phone down, but it was all a bit of a haze. Somehow, I managed to drive myself home and just bypassed all of the workmen we had around at the time and went straight up to my room. Saba had clocked that there was something seriously wrong and had realised she needed to get back home and very quickly she was there. To this day, I have no idea what happened to the workmen – I imagine Saba asked them to leave. Now I somehow had to tell her the news, when she was nine months pregnant, and due to give birth a week later.

How do you even begin to convey such devastating information to someone in that condition? "It's cancer." That's all I could say. Then there were more tears and we both just held each other. It wasn't long before she started wailing. Her head on the bed and so much pain in her face. It was like she had been stabbed in the gut. We have been together a long time and I had seen her cry before, but had never seen her wail like that. It was tough for me to take, to see Saba like that. It was one of the worst things I have ever seen in my life to be honest – because there was absolutely nothing I could about it, nothing I could say to make things better. For everything I was feeling, I also knew just how much this diagnosis was going to affect Saba and all the rest of my family.

I asked her if I she thought I had a chance, any chance, of beating this. But in truth, neither of us really knew. Then I had to call my mum but again, I don't think I could bring myself to tell her. I asked her if she was at work, I think I was crying again and she knew there was something wrong. She set off to come to see me and, because she had guessed things weren't good, she also called my dad and told him to do the same. When Mum got to the house, I was on the settee, with Saba sitting in the window seat. Somehow, I managed to tell her and, straightaway, she went white as a ghost. I remember her stepping backwards and almost falling over. She was stunned, completely stunned, and my sister Tayla was in bits, crying her eyes out.

They had had no idea there was anything wrong with me. They didn't have an inkling that anything was wrong and I hadn't even told them I had been going for tests. You never want to worry people, do you? Mum put her arm around me, she was trying to comfort me and tell me it was going to be alright, just like any mum would. But she didn't know and was in such a mess, a horrible nightmare. They left for a bit, to try and get some air and try and process what was going on and also because they didn't want me to see how upset they were. Then my Dad arrived.

He didn't cry or anything when I told him. He sat in his seat, motionless and expressionless. I don't think he could talk. I could see it just wasn't processing in his head. I know Dad so well that I could see he was really hurting, but he couldn't say a word. These were seriously tough moments, breaking the news to my family I had blood cancer and had no idea whether I was going to be alright. We probably all thought that was it and I was gone. How could we all be positive and think that I was going to get well again? None of us knew the truth.

It was staggering to think how life could be turned around in the space of a couple of hours. There I was, just going about my business, buying some paint, thinking I might have had a viral infection which would soon clear up and I'd be back in training in a couple of weeks. And now to this. The news I had cancer. It was surreal,scary and emotionally painful, all at the same time.

A very deep hole

I sent a message to my close friends to tell them the news. I couldn't face speaking to anyone else. Two of them, Adam and Robbie, turned up at the house. I kind of had to 'man up' in front of my mates. They could see I was upset but you can't cry in front of your boys now, can you? They were showing me their support and probably hiding what they really thought. I was trying to suppress how I felt and how worried I was about the diagnosis. We were sat in the kitchen, discussing what they could do to help and trying to think about what would happen next. Soon afterwards, Mila came back – Saba had taken her to her mum's to be out of the way – and that was another really difficult moment. She was in blissful ignorance without a clue what was going on and I kept looking at her, thinking she was going to grow up without her dad. I remember wondering: "How will she cope without me?" You hear of it all the time when children have to grow up without a parent. I didn't want Mila to have to go through that.

My mind was racing. I couldn't stop thinking about all the different scenarios. And, in those first few hours, I recall a feeling of 'I really don't deserve this.' Not really anger, more a case of 'Why me'? I wasn't a bad person, I don't do bad things to people, why should it be me having to deal with this? I kept thinking about my family, about Saba and Mila, and the baby who hadn't arrived yet. What it would be like for them with me no longer there was the main thing on my mind. I still didn't know what the treatment was going to entail or even when I would start it.

People often wonder how you can sleep after news like that, how you can even think about doing normal things and getting your head down to rest. I think I just passed out with exhaustion in the end, from everything that had gone on in this most horrible of days and the emotion of telling everyone I had cancer. I don't think I broke down again after that first day and those first few hours. I had my cry, I got it out of the way and that was it really.

From there, I just set about tackling the disease, getting all the information I needed to give myself the best chance of survival. I woke up the next morning and straightaway remembered everything that was happening and that, all of a sudden, everything had changed. I woke up thinking maybe it was a nightmare, but very quickly I knew that it wasn't. The reality was that yes, this really was happening to me and I had a long and very hard battle ahead. Make no mistake, I was in a very deep hole. I was right in the shit.

4

Chances with Wolves

Obviously there was nothing in my childhood that would ever compare to being told the news that I had blood cancer, but there were some tough times growing up. Football was so important to me, particularly, because I spent many of my childhood years in what could sometimes be a difficult neighbourhood.

My first junior team was Castlehurst Colts, then Chelmsley Ravens, where it was really good fun, with training in the week and matches on a Sunday. We used to train in Meriden Park in Chelmsley Wood and the team was run by Dave and Linda Bona, the parents of Paul, one of my mates from school. I mainly played in goal to start with, but always wanted to sneak out and play outfield. But, every time, it would be: 'Carl, get back in goal.' Maybe in the last game of the season, I'd be able to get out, play up front and try and grab some goals and some glory. We had a really good team in those days and Chelmsley was well known as an area for producing good footballers. Troy Deeney is a year younger than me but played for them and I knew him when we were growing up.

Paul was my close friend and he came to Wolves for a trial. Lee Vaughan, who went on to play professionally for Tranmere, Cheltenham and Kidderminster, was also there. I still think Bona thinks he is going to make it, even now!

Because we didn't have a car, the lady who made the tea used to pick us up to take us to the games and Mum and Dad would come along to watch. My mum still remembers one game when it was absolutely freezing and snowing horribly. I was in goal, had nothing to do and was pretty much in tears on the way home as I could hardly feel my hands.

There was a great feeling of togetherness around that team, playing with my mates. With the parents involved as well, just like in the local community, everyone looked out for each other. Although it was a great opportunity to join a Premier League Academy when I was spotted by Aston Villa, part of me felt sad that I had to stop playing for Chelmsley. I'd say I was at Villa from ten to maybe 12 or 13 and, looking back, my memories are very much about finding it difficult there. At that stage of my life, I found it all a bit too serious and I just didn't really enjoy the exprience. It was very competitive between everyone and quite cliquey, which Academies can be. My mum always talks about us going on the coach for a game against Manchester United, which then got postponed, so we stopped for breakfast on the way back. All the other lads were huddled together chatting and I was sat on my own. I didn't mind that as I was always more comfortable around people I knew, and was quite happy to be sitting alone. I didn't feel the need to act in a way that might get me involved or accepted.

Obviously I would always rather feel a part of things, but I have never been one who walks into a room and wants to be the centre of attention or make loads of friends. I have always tended to have only a few friends but really good friends, and that certainly wasn't the reason it didn't quite click for me at Villa. I just never felt completely comfortable or at home, but I kept going because it was Villa – they were my team and I was still proud to be in their Academy. It was a big step up from playing Sunday football but, more importantly, I was missing Chelmsley, my mates and all the fun we had. Obviously at Villa, I was playing in a team with some top players, like Gary Cahill and Luke Moore, but it just didn't feel like it was what I wanted to do. Chelmsley was my enjoyment and now that had gone. Even though Villa were coming up against teams like Manchester United and Chelsea and we were heading off to big tournaments, it just wasn't for me at that time. I'd be going back to school on a Monday and all my friends from school would be talking about the Chelmsley game from the weekend and I hadn't been involved.

Dad always had to find a way to get me to training at Villa, so he would have to call in a favour off someone. Even that made it difficult, compared to how easy it had been to get to the Chelmsley games. I remember coming back from Villa's Academy one day and just saying I didn't want to be there anymore. I told my mum and she spoke to my dad, who is a proper Villa fan, which is partly why I had carried on going for a bit longer when I wasn't enjoying it. I really didn't want to let him down. He would never put any pressure on me, but I think it meant a lot to him that I was there and, like all kids, I always wanted to try and make Dad proud. Anyway, we agreed I would leave, so I went back to Chelmsley in the Sunday league and was this time able to play up front. I was banging the goals in, maybe not overly prolific but I chipped in with my fair share. What a striker I was! I was quick and bigger than a lot of the lads of my age. I didn't have much skill or any mad tricks or anything, but I could certainly barge the defenders out of the way and get on the end of a through ball or two.

Again, in my head, I was thinking I was Ronaldo or Jay Jay Okocha, although the reality was very different. But I could hold my own up front and playing outfield improved my overall ability and my touch. That meant I became fairly decent with my feet, which has become more important for modern-day goalkeepers. I also think that playing street football on our estate, trying to score between two signposts, probably played a part in improving my footwork as well. So there I was, back at Chelmsley, really enjoying my football and once more looking forward to the weekends coming along. That quiet and fun life wasn't destined to last long.....

Soon, another Academy came calling. This time it was Wolves, although not in the way you might imagine. By this time Paul Bonar was on trial at Wolves, and noticed in the first week that there were two keepers. One was Dean Coleman, who would go on and play for Kidderminster and Walsall, and the other was someone they didn't seem to feel was going to make the grade. That meant Wolves were looking for another keeper and, while I can't completely remember how the conversation went, all of a sudden, one day I found myself sat in the Bona's car, on my way to a trial at Aldersley. It went well, they liked what they saw and I just carried on going.

Paul was signed as well and having him there was a huge help. It also meant I could get a lift from his parents, Linda or Dave. They were a massive help and influence on me growing up, with both the Sunday league team and then at Wolves, and I am still in close touch with them. The under-15s manager at Compton was Mike Smith and I felt at ease straightaway there and settled much quicker than I had at Villa. I fitted in and got on really well with everyone, so maybe I was also more prepared this time. The only different challenge here was perhaps a more important one. I was at a big club and a well-respected Academy, but I had arrived off the back of never having any proper goalkeeper training. Even at Villa, I don't remember having had too much specific work and, coming into Wolves, I certainly knew I needed to play catch-up.

All the other keepers around the age groups seemed to have been on the books a long time and, while athletically I was very good and I could pull off saves, I didn't really have any technical knowledge in the locker. Wolves could see I had some raw ability, which is why they took a chance on me, but I needed to 'up' my game in terms of the technical side. I remember we got to have one session with the then first-team keeper, Mike Stowell, but my knee locked and I was stretchered off. Typical! So much for making the most of my big chance to impress.

Little by little, I did improve towards the standard of the other keepers in terms of my understanding of the game tactically. I can still remember one game and one particular moment, which felt like a big breakthrough. We were playing Birmingham City at the Compton training ground and I was 14 or 15. I was confronted by a crowd of players, but smashed through a few opponents, caught the ball and thought: 'Yeh, I really enjoyed that!' I got a rush of adrenaline and felt ten foot tall, brimming with confidence. It kind of twigged that maybe I could do this goalkeeping stuff after all, that this could be it. And it was about more than just the fun of playing with my mates, at 'Wembley' outside our flats or on a Sunday for Chelmsley Ravens. I kept a clean sheet in that Birmingham game and it felt like a really important step for me.

I hadn't had the technical ability to start with but it was improving, alongside the fact I was strong and had that athleticism and half-decent instincts. Even then, when it came to the decision of who would get the scholarship, nothing was guaranteed. Dean Coleman was a local lad and a good keeper, and his dad was a good guy who seemed to get along really well with all the coaches. It was probably only natural to be thinking: 'They like Dean, he'll get a contract, maybe this isn't going to happen for me'. And yet, somehow, it did.

After the Christmas of that last year of training before I would either be released or kept on, I got a letter from Chris Evans, the Academy manager, telling me I'd got a three-year scholarship. How much was I buzzing at that news? It was brilliant. Having said that, it probably didn't do much for my schoolwork between receiving the letter and taking my GCSEs. I was always a little bit lively in school anyway. I wouldn't say I was naughty and I always turned up and tried to be respectful, but I did like a chat. I was also fairly laid-back and can't recall ever doing much homework or pushing myself academically. So, having been told in the January that I was going to be given a scholarship at a professional football club, work at school took a bit of a back seat and I didn't really revise for the exams.

Hindsight is a wonderful thing and, when I look back, I wish I had revised. I can't even remember my results. I think I got 4 C-grades and not much else. So it was not the best. But I knew that, in June, I was going to officially become a footballer and sign for Wolves, and that was a massively exciting prospect for any 15-year-old boy. Mum and Dad were happy and excited as well. I know my dad doesn't look too excited in the photograph of me signing all the forms but he definitely was. He is football-mad and I know what it meant to him for me to take that first major step on the ladder. After what had happened at Villa, he would have been forgiven for thinking I had blown my best chance. It was a great day, with a medical in the morning, getting changed in the dressing rooms and then an event in the evening where we signed the paperwork.

Mum and Dad were really happy I had a full-time occupation after leaving school, that everything I had done so far and everything we had all put into it now had an end goal. There was still a lot to strive for – to endeavour to go on and become a professional player. I wouldn't need to be hanging around the streets anymore, though. Football had given me a positive focus when I was a youngster and now it was giving me my first full-time job as well. It was also my first pay packet, of £55 a week; always a special moment for a kid growing up.

Not everyone was jumping for joy at the news, though. While my Dad was well into football, the rest of my Nigerian family didn't really understand it or grasp what it was that I was actually doing. I remember them speaking to my dad a lot and asking what it was that I was trying to achieve. When I speak to my aunties now about those times, it is quite funny because they might not admit it, but I know they were concerned. "What is this football nonsense?" they would ask my dad. "Why can't Carl read more books or go to school and then play football afterwards?"

They were academically trained and just couldn't understand it, thinking football was a hobby and a bit of fun that I should be doing in my spare time. Dad had to tell them it didn't really work like that and that I needed to take the opportunity which was on the table. They were living in Nigeria and America and didn't really understand that football is massive in this country and that I had taken the first step on the ladder to achieving something really big. My mum and her side of the family knew what a chance it was and obviously also my grandad, who I had spent so much time with growing up. He was buzzing, which was great for me to see, and it was just a shame that Teletext was no longer around for him to check our results if I did go on to make it! It was great when

I moved on to earn a little bit more than £55 a week, because that meant I could go shopping and help buy my grandad's groceries.

I was also really happy to have made my parents proud, as a lot of my success was in many ways down to them, and what I had learned from them growing up. Dad is a real man's man, he tells it like it is, and I think I got a lot of my physical attributes from him. But my mum was just as tough and so determined and mentally strong, which I think she passed on to me. She was really hard-working, spending hours and hours behind the counter of a local chip shop and she still does that now. Even when we moved to Stone, she would come back to Birmingham from Thursday to Sunday to work there while Dad looked after me.

I think your parents and indeed the surroundings you grow up in play a major part in moulding you into the person you become and I definitely took different bits of Mum and Dad's personalities into my life in football as I set off on what I hoped would be a successful career. And I know my Mum especially had been worried about what would happen if I didn't get the scholarship. I think she was pessimistic about my chances, more because she was just concerned that it might crush me if it didn't happen. But, to be honest, I had never really thought about trying to do anything else. I wasn't concentrating hard on my schoolwork as a back-up. There was nothing I wanted to do apart from be a footballer.

The only thing that did occasionally come to mind was the Army and I went for a week's work experience in Uxbridge. A lot of that was fitness-based, which I really enjoyed, so if I hadn't made it as a footballer maybe that could have been an option. Having said that, putting myself out there and potentially being shot at isn't something that has ever been high on my list of priorities. Football shots? Yes. Real life? No, thanks. So I was only really thinking about football. There was no Plan B, but that wasn't down to complacency or thinking it was definitely going to happen.

I was just working as hard as I possibly could at it and, if I didn't make it, only then would I move on to something else. I guess without any back-up plan, getting the scholarship was an even bigger moment, and I also think that my visualisations around that time played a part in getting that contract, and the more I used that approach in my career, the more it helped.

Even at that young age and although I hadn't experienced any of those moments involved with being a professional footballer, I had already seen them and played them out in my head. I had imagined what it would be like to perform in front of a big crowd, in that atmosphere and environment, and to make a save.

Obviously, it was very different seeing it all in my mind to actually delivering it in the flesh, but my imagination around football was unbelievable at that time. Kicking a ball around on that patch of land outside the block of flats in Castle Bromwich wasn't just our Wembley – it was 'the' Wembley to me. That visualisation and determination certainly helped me, but it could only get me so far. Now I had a scholarship and I was going to play the game full-time, with more expert coaching, more competitive games and more scrutiny and expectation.

I still had so much to do to achieve my dream of becoming a professional footballer and I was now heading into a spell of my career and my life which would mean so much, either good or bad. I couldn't wait to get started.

5

Heading to Christie's

If that feeling of anticipation waiting to go into my first season as a professional at Wolves was exciting, it couldn't have been more removed from what I thought and feared all those years later after being diagnosed with leukaemia. Having got that horrible and surreal first day out of the way, we got in very quickly to see the consultant Manos Nikolousis at the hospital. This was a chance for us to hear more about the disease first-hand and learn what was going to happen.

I think Manos had a shock when we walked in as he wouldn't have known how heavily pregnant Saba was. For my part, there was a real sense of uncertainty and nerves. I looked like I was strong. I suppose that's something I always did. Trying to be in control like I could handle anything. But I had a tight knot in my stomach which was filled with anxiety.

Manos quickly started giving us the information we needed to know. The questions anyone in that situation wants answered are not complicated: 'What are my survival chances? What it is looking like?' The answer from him was that there was between a 30 and 40 per cent chance of survival, which may not have been great for some people to hear. I was happy with that, though, and ready to accept that prognosis. In my head, when I first had that phone call in the car park, I thought I was gone. Finished. So as soon as I was told I had a chance, I knew I had to focus all my energies on what was ahead.

Manos then told us what the treatment would involve and the different options available. There was a lot to take in and Saba was having a hard time. She was in tears and when Manos mentioned that I would have to be in hospital for a month, she had to leave the room. A month seemed a very long time for a heavily pregnant woman who had just been through a rollercoaster of emotion. My stay turned out to be a whole lot longer. I think both Mum and Dad would rather have taken the illness than to see me affected and I remember my mum asking why it should happen to me when I was so young and fit. I remember answering: 'Why not me'? Black or white, big or small, rich or poor, cancer has no colours and can strike anyone at any time. It is indiscriminate. Maybe it should happen to me as I had been so blessed in so many other ways.

We were all still shell-shocked to be honest and all those questions were going through our minds. But at least now we had an idea what we were dealing with. Then the news had to be announced publicly. I remember being in touch with Wolves and hearing that it was going to be released at 5pm on that Thursday, with the staff and players being told just before. It was very strange waiting for it to be announced and thinking my phone was going to be very busy all of a sudden once the announcement hit social media.

I am never one who likes being the centre of attention. I'm generally happy keeping myself to myself but I realised this was going to blow up when the news got out. I use social media, but not too much, and it has always been mainly as a tool to speak to supporters or about my other interests, like boxing. It has never been something I have used to show off anything about my life. I sensed it was going to be big on social media but the one thing I was most concerned about was not becoming an 'RIP' hashtag.

It is mad how your mind works in those situations and the things you think about. I had a lot of messages and well-wishes, which was great, but at the same time they were difficult to deal with because I didn't really know what was happening. I couldn't reply to anyone and say more because I had no idea what the next few months had in store.

Saba was only a week or so from her due date and Manos gave me the opportunity to delay starting the treatment. But we agreed I should start as soon as possible. That was what I wanted. I didn't want to be waiting. I wished to give myself the best possible chance of being around for the baby and Mila later in life. That felt more important than being there for the birth but potentially reducing my long-term survival prospects. Delaying even for one day was not an option for me – with everything going on in my head, I couldn't just sit there waiting. Very quickly, I went back to hospital, Heartlands in Birmingham, and I was ready. Ready to fight this for me and my family, so I would be able to spend the rest of my life with them.

I remember thinking I wouldn't mind being homeless on the street as long as I could just witness my children growing up. My spirits were lifted when, before very long, I had a visitor at the hospital – the former Aston Villa player Stiliyan Petrov. 'Stan' had previously been successfully treated for acute lymphoblastic leukaemia (ALL), which was exactly the type of blood cancer I had been diagnosed with. I know Gabby Agbonlahor really well and Stan got my number off him and said he wanted to come and see me. His visit, particularly at that time, was a massive help. Having had leukaemia himself, he understood what I was about to go through and could tell me precisely what side-effects I could suffer. Also, being in the same profession, he had a grasp of all the extra attention that went around it. He was good as well with advice as we were quickly having to decide on different options for treatment, in particular which hospital to go to.

I had started out at Heartlands but many people were recommending Christie's in Manchester as one worth looking into. Heartlands is very good but it was very close to where I had grown up and, to be honest, I just wanted to be somewhere else, out of the way. At Heartlands, it was possible I would be walking past people in the corridor I knew. Even now, every time I go to the hospital, I see someone I know. That just wasn't something I needed when I was dealing with what had been thrown at me. Without wanting to sound rude, I knew I was going to go through some tough times and having to make the effort to speak to people and chat about old times was better avoided. In Manchester, I would be much more out of the way and able to get my head down and proceed with the treatment. So I started at Heartlands, then moved up to Christie's quite quickly.

By this time, my mood was starting to become more positive. Having had the 30-40 per cent shout from Manos and then meeting Stan, who had come through his own battle, I had a good, positive impetus. The tears had gone. Now it was time to get to work. Time to tick off the treatment and beat this thing I had in front of me. I also had a lift from Molineux at this point. During a time when I was able to grab a few hours at home, the Wolves captain Danny Batth came to see me and said the players had been told the news about me in the dressing room by the head coach, Nuno. It had come as a huge shock to all of them, they had no idea that what I had been suffering from was so serious. Exactly the same as how I felt before hearing that diagnosis.

All that the lads knew was that I had been off for a while but that I was due back soon. Danny told me he was in tears when he was told and that he hadn't cried since he was 11. I am really close to him and that brought it all home to me again. I remember we both put photos on Twitter, as I wanted to say thank-you to people for all their messages and I wanted to tell everyone I was ready to give it my all. I have also thought a lot about the Wolves doctor, Matt Perry, and how difficult it must have been for him to make that phone call. Maybe he had an inkling before about what it might be, I don't know, but it must have been tough for him to put me in the picture, even if it is something he was used to doing as part of his job. He was someone I spoke to as we were choosing hospitals for my treatment.

More support came from my auntie, Elizabeth Anionwu, an incredible lady who became the first sickle cell nurse specialist in Britain and has gone on to become a Dame. She is always someone I enjoy talking to and this was a particularly important time to ask her advice. She also recommended Christie's. It made sense as it's the biggest cancer hospital in Europe and was far enough from Wolverhampton and Birmingham to be out of the way but close enough for family and friends to come back and forth.

The amount of good wishes I was receiving was almost overwhelming but I massively appreciated the support and it was heartening to know that so many people, in football and life in general, were looking out for me. I thought it was important to thank them, even though I needed to make sure I didn't get too consumed in it all. I knew my main focus had to be in getting through what I was going to have to get through, and so while I definitely felt all of that support and appreciated it, I couldn't afford to be too consumed by it. The focus had to be more on wanting to get better, so I would be able to thank everyone.

Having said that, once the treatment began and things settled down after the initial announcement, it was always really nice to read those messages. They gave me a boost during some very difficult times. Even maybe six months into my treatment, I would still be receiving them and they really did help. I could never really say how I was doing. I obviously knew more than I sometimes said, but I was never comfortable in saying I was going to be okay.

So I did need and appreciate that support but, more than anything, I was making sure I was concentrating on the treatment and doing everything I could to help myself. I never once googled anything to do with leukaemia. I didn't think it would help me, although I know Saba was looking on the internet. That was probably a natural reaction. I didn't want to look at too much information which might have confused me.I was getting mine from far better sources than Google – from Manos, from Stan, and from other medical people. It was all about trying to learn about the things I could actually control and not necessarily the disease itself or the treatment, which I couldn't really do anything about. I read up on what my diet should be, for example, and how I could improve that, even though it was already something I was fairly careful about.

So what could I do with the tools that I could control that might be able to help in my recovery? Things like diet, exercise through walking and looking after my mental state. I decided to go vegan, looking into herbal remedies such as Dr Sebi, a diet which aims to help your body heal. I also remember saying to Saba early on that I would never, ever quit. If the disease was going to beat me, it might beat my body, but it would never, ever beat my mind. That I was absolutely sure of.

Anyone who knows me knows exactly what my mind is like. Mentally, I was going to be fighting every inch of the way. My body might let me down but my mind? No chance. That strength was a real comfort in those first few days. I have always had the mentality of never wanting to quit and, however hard it was going to be, I knew the state of my mind wouldn't be a problem.

Aside from all the emotional issues and talking about treatment options, there were practical things to deal with. I had always been taught to be careful about money and to be suspicious of other people and what their motives might be. When I meet new people, I am very careful until I really get to know them. By now, I had been with Saba a long time but hadn't got round to putting everything in our joint names. We weren't married and I was worried about what might happen to her if things went badly. What did I have to do to make sure I could give her everything I had, if I didn't actually recover? Our house was in my name, as well as a couple of other properties I had. And all of a sudden, with this life-threatening diagnosis, I realised money doesn't mean a great deal. Other things in life are way more important.

I rang financial advisers and our mortgage people to find out what I could do to pass everything on. I wanted to get some money into her bank so, if anything happened to me, she could get by until she maybe needed to sell the house or remortgage. She needed to have everything that was mine, to keep her and the kids going. It sometimes takes a development like this to make you realise what really is important and, while I wasn't a millionaire, everything I had needed to go to her.

Once I had decided to go up to Christie's, making sure I had an apartment not far from the hospital became another priority. Having to attend to the practical things doesn't go away even while you are concentrating on trying to tackle such a serious illness. I was in Heartlands having steroids for maybe a week before moving to Manchester. From there, I knew it was time to crack on with getting this disease beaten.

I remember when we first met Manos, he gave me a piece of paper with some information on about the treatment. I passed it straight to my mum for her to look at and she asked him: "Is this my guarantee that you are going to make my son better?" Quick as a flash, he said he would and that was a real comfort to Mum, who had been really worried about whether I would survive. She was always something of a Daddy's girl and told me that when she lost her dad, she poured everything she had into bringing me up. She can still remember me coming up the drive in a green coat and red bobble hat not long after he had passed away and thinking: 'That is why I am living'.

Her dad, my grandad, had also been treated at Heartlands for cancer, so maybe some of those memories were coming back as well. So while Mum felt she was being selfish in thinking of herself and what she might do if I didn't make it, I could totally understand her having those dark thoughts because we have always had such a close bond.

I couldn't let her down now, could I?

6

Making the grade

As well as looking out for me when I had leukaemia, Mum had always been a big influence on me growing up. So, heading into my Academy scholarship at Wolves, I was pleased I could carry on living at home in Birmingham and travel in each day. I didn't want to be in digs and the journey wasn't too bad on a couple of buses and the Metro or train.

My friend, Paul Bona, had been released, which was a big disappointment for him. His family had also been great for me with lifts to training and after he had left, it sometimes made it difficult for me to get across. I could only really afford to go to training once a week and never had any sort of proper goalkeeping coaching. But once I began the scholarship, that all changed, as I was being paid and had a travel allowance, so I could in effect use a bus pass to make the journey to Wolverhampton.

I started off using the Metro. When the allowance went up, I was able to take the train. To be fair, though, I wasn't really paying for either. Someone was knocking out fake bus and train passes and I was there, first in the queue. I'd get on the bus, a quick flash of the pass to the driver and then walk on fast. It saved me an extra £50 a month, which was a lot to someone earning £55 a week. I was buzzing.

Sometimes, there were issues with public transport and I had to run from the station to Molineux to make sure I was in on time. But I definitely preferred it that way than being in digs and I'd meet up with Lewis Gobern and Marlon Walters, who both lived in Birmingham, so we could travel across together. It was down to me to be up early in the morning and make sure I was on time. To have that discipline, at a young age, was a good way for me to learn. There were a few times when I was late, some of which were within my control, such as snatching an extra ten-minute snooze, and some which weren't. Instilling that discipline and structure was important early in my career because often, unless you go to college or university, you don't have the discipline at a young age of having to make sure you look after yourself properly.

Keith Downing, my first manager when I was a scholar at Wolves, was absolutely fantastic. He did everything for us, including driving the minibus from where we met at Molineux first thing in a morning, down to training at Compton. The year above my age group was something of a golden year for scholars with people like Lewis, Nathan Talbot and Ashley Vincent – they had a really good team. Our age group, the under-17s, weren't expected to do all that much but we started really well and went on to have a decent season.

Keith is a great coach and has gone on to achieve a lot both at club level and with England junior teams since starting out in the Academy at Wolves. But he doesn't half have a switch that he can press if people mess about and don't do things properly. As I got to know more about him, I remember being told the fans used to call him 'Psycho' because of his tackling and no-nonsense approach as a player. Having worked under him as a coach, it's fair to say I could see why. He was generally mildly spoken and very articulate in getting his messages across. But when he 'went' and actually lost it…oh my God! I've never been scared of much but I never wanted to get on the wrong side of Keith. Or Psycho!

I don't think I ever copped one of his bollockings on an individual basis but can recall a few as a group. Once, we were messing about in training, with Leon Clarke, I think, engineering much of the mischief. "Leon, fuck off to the bus now, go and sit on the fucking bus," Keith boomed. He continued the session but still wasn't happy with our attitude, so we were all sent off to the bus, driven to Molineux, then back for more training in the afternoon. That was always a wounder, as it meant we would be travelling home at the end of that extra session in the rush hour. We went back to Compton in the afternoon and this time it was for a load of running. This was our punishment.

So while Keith is a great guy and always so professional and mild-mannered when you meet him, he had that switch and was able to instil discipline in all of us, which is what you always have to do as a coach. He provided a perfect introduction to full-time football for me, and for any young pro. His sessions were brilliant. We knew we had to be 'on it' and work hard, otherwise we'd be on the end of that 'Psycho' switch. But I always loved training so, for me, doing it every day was absolutely perfect.

It was the technical part of goalkeeping I really needed to learn and that is what I found most difficult. I was good in the games, I could be effective but the technical side was what I was lacking and needed to improve. But they were great times in the Academy, fun times along with the hard work. Times you remember really fondly when you look back.

There were lads in our group from all over the place – local lads, some from different parts of England and a fair few from Ireland. It was a good mix, which made for fun in the dressing room, with the banter going on between everyone. I did have to get used to the 'Your Mum' shouts from the Irish lads, though, which is a piss-take referring to people's mums. Where I had come from, saying that was pretty much straight fighting talk, so I had to adjust to the fact it was part of the banter and they didn't really mean it. If I reacted in the dressing room in the same way as I did growing up – in fact all of the lads - we'd have been fighting non-stop and wouldn't have had time to play football!

I really enjoyed those days in the Academy and it was never a burden to get up early and go into training. So many young boys want to play football every day, don't they? I was one of them and it was such a privilege. There was never a day when I thought I couldn't do it or I couldn't be bothered. I have always enjoyed working hard.

As I got going into the second year of my scholarship, I had developed more 'know-how' about training, what to expect and what being a footballer was all about. Even in that summer, between the first and second years, I kept myself super-fit. I knew what I needed to do to keep myself in the best possible shape and give myself an opportunity to land that coveted professional contract. I think those days paved the way for what became my obsessive training behaviour throughout the rest of my career. Every now and again, we were fortunate enough to go and train with the first-team keepers, like Matt Murray and Michael Oakes, who were always spot-on for me. Sure enough, everyone would eventually start calling me 'Mini Matty' and I know fans have since made up a song to compare the two of us! Fortunately for me, Matty went on to become a really close friend as well as a positive role model as I was starting out.

As I turned 17, I found myself involved with the first team a bit more. And a lot of the senior players took me under their wing to help me along. Dean Sturridge was a Birmingham lad who knew a few people from my area, Shaun Newton was good, and so too was George Ndah, who had a Nigeria link. My dad said I'd be able to trust George with anything and he felt comfortable knowing George was there and would be on hand to help me if needed. Lee Naylor is another one I would chat to and, as with all young players, the closer you get to the first team, the more the senior players start to know who you are.

I had already started doing fitness sessions with Matty and George. They dragged me along to the gym and showed me what was required to stay in shape above and beyond training. When I saw them going to the gym and the dedication they were showing, it made me realise that was what I needed to do as well. Some of the other first-teamers were often tough on me but all these influences and experiences gave me things to learn and advice I could put into practice to improve.

As time went on, I also managed to get myself a car, a nice little Corsa. To be honest, and this is confession time, I used to do a bit of unofficial driving after starting my lessons but before I had passed my test. Mum would be working on a Friday and a Saturday night and Dad would go to the pub, so I waited until he was there and then took the car out for a little spin around the estate. I passed my test and later moved on to a Rover, which looked the business, but was absolutely rubbish. Things were always going wrong with it and eventually I managed to save up enough to buy an old BMW, which kept me going for a few years.

So things were good, although that's not to say I didn't escape the odd bit of 'tough love' as I was coming through the ranks. The gym used to be next to the away changing room at Molineux, with the office of manager Dave Jones at the top of the corridor. The one day, I walked into the gym in the morning with a cup of tea and was very quickly called into Dave's office and given a proper and thorough bollocking. Taking a hot drink in was not the done thing, although he did tell me in the middle of the tirade that I was getting the brunt of his bad morning! Needless to say, never again did I work out, with a cuppa close to hand. Actually, I don't think I went to the gym for a couple of days after that just to be safe and everyone knows how much I love that place. I didn't even want to walk past Dave's office for a while to be fair.

But so much of what a manager does in those early years is about trying to keep you on your toes and ensure you stay motivated. I remember when I signed my first professional contract and got given three years, Dave said he would have given me two and then just walked off. He was certainly trying to keep me in my place. I have seen him more recently and he tells me he always knew I would make it, although it didn't feel that way for me at the time. Managers use many different techniques to push players and get the best out of them, and that was what Dave was doing with me. Just making sure I didn't take any liberties or take things for granted, he was keeping my standards high.

Dave was another manager at Wolves who did well and played a key part in the club's recent history, getting them back to the top flight after such a long absence. I know we didn't stay in the Premier League but to get up that season was great and the play-off final win over Sheffield United in Cardiff gave thousands of fans so many fantastic memories.

It is sometimes a fine line with managers in those situations when you have a falling-out. I have always had respect for people and been able to take criticism. I was certainly not going to answer Dave back and it wouldn't have been sensible to start arguing with him at 16 or 17. That's not to say I wasn't comfortable with confrontation. I remember once, when I was very young and training with the first team now and again, that there was an issue with Paul Ince. He used to hammer the kids, probably to try and toughen them up, and this one time I was in his team for a small-sided game. He blamed me for conceding a goal and I snapped. I'd had enough and just thought: 'Fuck it, he's not speaking to me like this anymore!' So I took my gloves off, walked over to him and said: "Who the fuck do you think you are you talking to?" As ever, other players stepped in. Nothing major happened, and everything went calm. I was a big lad even then, so I'm not sure Incey fancied it to be honest! But, after that, I have to say he was absolutely brilliant with me. He helped me a lot – maybe he had a lot more respect for me because he had seen I was prepared to stick up for myself.

So, yes, I always respected everyone but if there was something I felt needed to be said, I wouldn't hold back. That's how it should be and, in my experience, most people, even managers, appreciate that honesty and feedback as long as it is done right. I never had many set-to's with managers but had many grown-up discussions. I once had a go with Dean Saunders – much more about that later – but for most of the time, even if I disagreed with a manager, it would be expressed in adult conversations. I'd let them know I wasn't happy and be pissed off for a few days but after that it would be a case of getting on with it.

The way I saw it with managers, we were both men, both able to say what we thought, then shake hands and move on. It is always my attitude that, even if I don't agree with you, I will respect you. There was the situation with Kenny Jackett when I was dropped, which I will also go more into later, but I would still say I have massive respect for Kenny. I didn't agree with his decision to drop me, I wasn't happy and still don't think it should have happened, but I would say I never lost respect for him. The way managers deal with players is linked to how people should treat each other generally. As long as you are straight and honest and they are straight and honest with you, you can respect their truth even if you disagree with it. That is exactly how I'd describe that situation with Kenny.

In life, as in football, I would like to think that I am always myself. Even if you don't agree with me, if you can accept that I am telling you the truth from my point of view, that is fine and I am comfortable with that. I always prefer people telling me what they are thinking even if I don't agree, rather than hide things or go around the truth. It is always best to get it out there, so if a manager is going to drop me, just tell me the reason. And as long as I can see that is your truth, even if I don't agree with it, I will respect it.

I always tried to give that back to people from my point of view but being straight and honest isn't always the case in a dressing room. There is a lot that goes on that can push the boundaries, when it comes to being truthful. When I look back over my Wolves career and the relationships with managers and being in and out of the team, I always think I found my way in somehow. Once I worked myself in and had the spot, I was quite hard to move out of the way. That was the feeling I always kept and it made sure I stayed motivated during any difficult periods.

We had some great keepers during my time at Wolves, from Matt Murray when I was coming through to Wayne Hennessey, who played more often than not when we were competing for a place. Then there were Dorus De Vries, Tomasz Kuszczak, Emi Martinez, Azza (Aaron McCarey) and Lonners (Andy Lonergan). Somehow, on a regular basis, I managed to get myself in. I was always confident in my own ability and in the back of my mind had this belief that I could perform if I was given the chance. And, once I was in, I was confident I could stay in. That was what I always went back to when there was discussion about which goalkeeper was going to play and whether I was going to be involved. I always felt that, somehow, by hook or by crook, I would play.

Like most players you speak to, though, I would always say I wish I had played more. Of my 274 career appearances, 207 were for Wolves and, even though I had one or two injuries to contend with, I'd love that number to have been higher. That's me I guess, always pushing myself, always striving to make the very most of any opportunities I received.

7

Support from Nigeria

That determination to be the best I could be and make the most of every opportunity, was something that extended well beyond just me. There are several other members of my family who, in their chosen careers, have been far more successful than I have.

My Nigerian heritage was massive for me and it has always been really important. And, among all the support I had during my treatment, especially in those early stages, the Nigerian side of my family were right behind me, sending me messages. I have already mentioned that Auntie Elizabeth – Dame Elizabeth Anionwu to give her full title – was someone I was very proud of and someone whose advice I had sought about where to be treated. She had recommended Christie's, then came to see me early on once I was settled in. I wasn't mad for visitors throughout the treatment really, especially if I was struggling, but Elizabeth is quite persistent. And she was in Manchester doing a talk, so it worked out quite well. I wasn't going to say no to a Dame coming to see me, was I?

Her work has been incredible and we are all so very proud of her. I remember Dad telling me about her when I was young but it was only when I grew up that I really understood it and got to realise she was so prominent in founding something for sickle cell patients which helped with a disease my Grandad suffered from, as well as other friends. Elizabeth came to see me a couple of times and brought another auntie, Titi Ikeme, while Auntie Joy from America was another visitor. Given she had come so far, I couldn't really say no. She would have broken the door down if I had.

In Nigerian culture, you have aunties in your family but you also tend to call family friends aunts as well. Hence, I had a lot of aunties. Vicky, Ozena,

Maureen, Joy, Obie, Chinwe, Nkiru – both in London and in America I have so many of them who I used to see and have had as a big part of my life. Many of them wanted to come and see me but would have had to plan it for a fair while given the distance involved. So Dad tried to put a lot of them off as, without knowing how I would be feeling the day they wanted to come, it was very difficult to look too far ahead.

It was always good to see them when I could – I love all my Aunties and spent a lot of time with them as a kid. Auntie Vicky lived in London and I have great memories of going to see them as a family. We couldn't afford the train, so we'd go on the National Express coach from Birmingham to Victoria and it felt like it took absolutely ages. From Victoria, we'd get the bus to Elephant & Castle and that is when I knew we were close to reaching my auntie's house. I had a lot of cousins and there always seemed to be a reason to be in London seeing our family. We'd just hang out for the weekend, watch some telly, just do kids' stuff, eating food, staying out of the way of the adults as much as we could.

Food was a big part of the culture as well. Wherever you go and get Nigerian hospitality, there is a constant supply of food. That was the same in Nigeria, where I went a few times while growing up. We would visit different family members and there would always be something to eat from one house to the next. "Here, have something to eat." "I've just had some Jollof rice." "Well, have some more and have some soup as well…" Great memories!

Grandad, who had moved to England and was followed by my Dad, took me to Nigeria for the first time when I was nine. Dad's mum had passed away when he was young and he wanted me to see Nigeria and go to the village, Onitsha, where he was born. It was 76 Upper Newmarket Road. I'll never ever forget that address. I met Dad's sister during that visit, in her kitchenette, and life was very different out there, including the water system. To shower, you'd fill a bucket with hot water from cups. Even when Grandad was back in Birmingham, he would have a bucket in the bathroom for that reason and I bet if I went to Auntie Vicky's even now, she would have the bucket, too.

It is so mad what you remember from when you were younger but that was one of the things and I would love to take my kids over when they are a bit older, so they too can get to understand the culture of the country. I actually got stuck over there with Grandad as he couldn't come back due to some reasons linked with immigration. I think he had used Dad's passport to get over there if I'm honest. I still have no idea how he got away with that! It was a bit more dangerous than me and my dodgy travel pass to get over to Academy training!

We ran out of money as well and ended up staying in a hotel in Lagos because my uncle, who was quite successful in politics over there, helped us out. Grandad wasn't able to come back for a while, so I had to travel back on my own, with a few people helping me on the journey. You could say my mum was panicking about whether I would get home, especially as she didn't want me to go in the first place. It was a mad experience but one I enjoyed and will always remember.

I know there can be dangers in Nigeria but I don't believe Africa is the place it is portrayed as in the media and it will always be such a huge part of my life. It is a country I love and I always will.

I also have some very successful family members on the Nigerian side, as well as Elizabeth. Charles Venn and Azuka Oforka have made it in the acting world and have both most recently starred in Casualty. Charles has really progressed massively, probably over the last seven or eight years, and it has been great to see him come through almost from nowhere having worked so hard. I used to see plenty of Charles in London when I was younger. He is a little older than me and my dad looked after him from time to time. I think he thought my Dad was pretty strict with him, like he was with all of us.

I remember Charles being a male model and saw his picture in a magazine one day when I was at his house. I was amazed. This meant he had made it but, for me even now, I see him as Charles my cousin and not Charles the actor. I remember him first on Footballers' Wives and then he went onto EastEnders and that is where I really thought he had cracked it – EastEnders is mainstream! More recently, he has become one of the main guys on Casualty as well as making an appearance on Strictly Come Dancing. I always knew he had some rhythm! It hasn't come easy for him – he has been grinding for a long, long time, and the success didn't come overnight. I am madly proud of him and everything he has done; the same with Azuka, who is Elizabeth's daughter, and also had a few years on Casualty as one of the nurses, Louise. I was aware of her and what she was doing but we hadn't really met until an awards ceremony we were all attending in Birmingham when Charles introduced us by saying: "Carl, here is another of your cousins." Azuka has done really well, too, and it is quite mad to stop and think that the three of us have all managed to achieve something in our chosen careers, although I still don't think any of it compares to Elizabeth's accomplishments.

Towards the end of 2019, Elizabeth received a Lifetime Achievement Award at the Pride of Britain awards, presented by Janet Jackson. We are all so proud of her and what she has achieved.

As I have said before, with Mum and Dad splitting up when I was young, our family life wasn't the traditional sort but everyone still gets on and the same goes for Mum's side of the family. When I was younger and Mum was working at a chip shop, I spent a lot of time at her mum's. She would drop me at Nan's on a Friday and Saturday and I have to say, in the nicest possible sense of the word, that Nan really is crackers. Eventually, she moved to Devon, which is where I remember our first holidays and which I probably didn't appreciate then. I'd love to go back to that time, just to make sure I appreciated it more, spending time together by the sea.

Nan is back in the West Midlands now, living with her partner Mike – my step-grandad – in Erdington. I have to say Nan is bullet-proof; one tough woman! She has a pacemaker and once broke her ankle really badly but you don't keep her down for long. So many nans are really strong, aren't they? Almost untouchable. Mum and Nan had a great relationship but, like all mothers and daughters, had their moments, especially at Christmas. It's a scene so many will identify with, spending Christmas Day together with the family and having a few drinks – more than a few drinks, in fact!

Nan was lively enough at the best of times but we would always be like 'wait for it' and she'd start! She would start telling Mum that she had brought me up because I spent so much time with her at weekends. She liked to think of herself as some sort of Mother Teresa character, helping to bring everyone up. Mum would give a bit back and all hell would break loose. A classic festive argument. All would be forgotten by the end of the night or next morning. It would be the same story every Christmas.

Family was very important and we also had my Uncle John, Mum's brother, live with us for a bit after Nan moved to Devon. Although he was my uncle, he was only seven years older than me and I have to say I was a right little shit in my behaviour to him. When I was seven or eight and he was a teenager, I remember I used to punch him and run off. Good times! This was the dynamic of the family on all sides. People would forever be popping in or staying, even living with us. There always seemed to be a stray cousin or a stray auntie who would come and live with us for a while and there wasn't much room in the house to start with.

I still see Nan and Uncle John quite a bit as they live close but I don't get to see my auntie much which is a shame, although it is nice to pick up the phone and talk. I appreciate that support network and find it useful to have people out there that I can ask questions of. When I was younger, I probably thought I knew it all and didn't ask the opinions of others. That was stupid really. Family members always have your best interests at heart and are usually knowledgable, so it's great to be able to use them as a sounding board which is what I do a lot of now.

I spoke to Elizabeth about what I needed to do to get back to full health and to feel fit again as I was coming through my treatment. But like most families, we probably only really get together at the usual events like weddings, christenings and funerals. So often it is a case of waiting for one of those occasions to come along, then you can all be together and see how things are going. With our family, there is always a lot to catch up on. A lot of my aunties didn't grasp how important football was going to be for me as a career, purely because it wasn't something they completely understood. Yet just as they were always there for me and supporting me all the way with my illness, so too they were in my football, once they could see the potential that was there.

8

Striving to improve

Although I knew my family would be there to support my career, having to wait and show patience was a key factor in the early days. I was just looking for that opportunity to show what I could do. The 2003/04 season, when Wolves were in the Premier League, gave me my first taste of being in a match-day squad at the age of just 17. The first game I was on the bench for was the Carling Cup win against Burnley and I was there again for matches straight afterwards against Middlesbrough and Birmingham.

I had a few more appearances among the substitutes in the New Year, including that great few days when we beat Manchester United at Molineux and followed up with a home draw against Liverpool. It was a strange time because, while I have always been a confident character, this was the Premier League and I was still very young. I might have been confident but I'm not really sure I would have been been able to hold my own in a Premier League match then. You always need to have confidence and back your ability in football, but the truth is that I was not ready to play in the top division.

Getting into the match-day squad at a young age is a time when you just get on with everything quietly and mind your own business. Get into the dressing room and sit there and read your programme, only speak if you are spoken to. Don't leave your seat much and don't go in the physio room. It would never cross my mind to have a massage. That would have been taking the piss! That would lead to a heap of trouble if the first-team lads thought you were getting ideas above your station.

A fair few of the senior players were very good to me as I was learning the trade, including Matty Murray, Michael Oakes and the goalkeeping coach, Bobby Mimms. Even so, it would have been a big ask if my League debut had come as a teenage goalkeeper in that unforgiving environment. Did it nearly happen? On one occasion, it did. It was the game at Middlesbrough, which was lively enough as it happened as Alex Rae was sent off and Paul Butler was waiting for Danny Mills in the tunnel afterwards. Just the usual stuff! Oakesey went down during play and, to be honest, I absolutely shit myself.

It's a crazy feeling when you are in that situation as a young player, potentially about to go on such a massive stage. Your gut drops and all your senses become heightened. I remember my arms and legs were shaking and my mind was saying: 'Shit! you're really going on', along with repeats of: 'You can do this'. The battle of the mind had begun. I certainly was not technically ready but obviously if it had happened that Oakesey didn't recover, I would have gone out there and given it my best shot. Everything happens for a reason and the experience of those seven or so games when I was on the bench that season certainly helped me in the future.

Despite my self-doubts, to have been elevated to the squad improved my confidence again and helped me progress that little bit further, in the same way as training with the first team did. Whenever you train with better players, you might not even notice or realise it is helping you at the time but it does push you. My first taste of senior football when it did arrive was on loan, in the Conference, with Accrington Stanley. Exactly! By this time, I was 18 and my first appearance was away to Aldershot on October 16, 2004, in front of just under 3,000. It was quite a baptism.

As an Academy player, you are pampered a fair bit with a lot of tasks done for you – kit provided, food, all the things you come to expect as being normal. And you would always be provided with slips or sloggies, which give added protection during a game in a certain gentleman's area! Well, I turned up to Accrington with just my boots and, lo and behold, there were no sloggies. I was wearing boxer shorts, which I wanted to keep for the journey home but, what the hell, I had to wear them for the game. Sure enough, in the first minute, bang! There was a 50-50 to go for with Aldershot striker Aaron McLean and I was studded in that very private area. Wow, that was sore! Especially without the protection of slips or sloggies which I was used to at Wolves. With a big gash, I still had two other 'balls' to protect on the pitch, and at least the right gear would have helped with any unnecessary movement.

It was some welcome to senior football. A very painful one. I was in agony. We got to half-time and someone handed me their used slips. Not the best gift I have ever received but I didn't care, I had to wear them. I was in so much pain. I went back out there, finished the game and was pleased to keep a clean sheet in a goalless draw. So that was a start.

Bobby Mimms phoned me after the game – I didn't even know he had been there – and said: 'Fair play'. He thought it was one hell of a whack I had taken so early on. You weren't wrong, Bob! I played three more games for Accrington which ended in two defeats and another goalless draw. I wouldn't necessarily say I enjoyed that spell but I was off and running and had a taste of senior football and some more vital experience in the locker.

I stayed in a bed and breakfast while I was there and couldn't get hold of much healthy food. There were loads of chippies and Chinese takeaways in the local area and the night before my debut, I remember walking to an Indian restaurant as there wasn't any food available where I was staying. I can't remember what I ordered but I'm sure it wasn't ideal. Even at that level, you don't find many players preparing for their senior debut by sticking away a curry the night before!

It taught me to appreciate everything I had at Wolves and that was the same with my next loan spell, at Stockport County the following season in League Two. I played nine games in the September and October, we only won one of them and we lost my last one 6-0 at Carlisle. It was more good experience and all part of the learning process but, no disrespect to Stockport or Accrington, it was a real eye-opener about what football was like at the lower levels. Everything about their facilities was different to Wolves and it proper put a rocket up my backside and made me realise how fortunate I was and how I had to do everything within my power to make the grade at Molineux.

It gave me that added kick-start to work harder, always work harder. That was the only way it was going to happen for me. Yes, I always worked hard and gave my best but those loan spells told me it was time to find another gear to move up to. And that was the catalyst for me to push on again. I always feel that, throughout my career, the only reason I kept up my levels was because I never ever rested on my laurels. I was always looking to do more, whether that was extra work on the training pitch, in the gym, or in other areas, such as taking up yoga.

My mate Jamie Reynolds runs the Velocity gym in Birmingham and I'd be going there twice a week on top of what I was doing at Wolves. It was outside of my football training and the club didn't always like it but they realised why I went. Jamie has worked with a lot of top sportsmen, especially boxers, including Anthony Joshua.

When I was younger, I also used to go to a boxing gym with a few of my mates. We thought we were tough but, when we got there, we all realised we weren't as tough as we thought. As a teenager, I would go to a gym called Birmingham Irish in Lea Village, which would keep me fit as I was starting out in football. I'd be down there training, someone would ask me if I wanted to spar and I'd be like, gumshield in, let's go!

I'd go for a couple of months, stop for a bit and pick it up again. There was also a time when I was at Wolves and not really playing so I'd go there and train at the weekend as well. Boxing is something I've picked up a bit more recently, maybe once a week, just to help keep myself in shape. It is a sport that has always fascinated me and I love watching it. The fitness levels of boxers is incredible but you add to that the skill and their mindset and it is an amazing sport. I remember it being on in the house when I was younger, watching the likes of Prince Naseem Hamed and once staying up with Dad for Mike Tyson against Frank Bruno. It was the second time they had fought and Bruno lost again, so I was devastated. I loved Bruno and loved Tyson as well but I had wanted Bruno to win.

The Nigel Benn and Chris Eubank era was great as well when I was growing up in the 1990s and I'd always be watching at home with Dad, probably on some dodgy cable box. I watch old fights on You Tube as well, such as ones involving Roberto Duran, Sugar Ray Leonard, Thomas Hearns and Marvin Hagler. And the best sportsman that has ever lived for me was a boxer, the one and only Muhammed Ali. Boxing was always my second sport and Ali has always been my hero. He has eclipsed any footballer for me. It was not just his boxing ability but how he handled himself outside the ring and everything he stood for. For me, he is the biggest sportsman that has ever lived and possibly always will be.

My interest in fitness had always been there. I enjoy it and it became a routine during my career. That worked well because when you stand still in football, that is effectively going backwards. There are always talented young players coming through and I always felt that if I could stay fitter and stronger than them, they weren't going to take my place. I always kept that mentality of trying to stay ahead and, at the same time, picking up bits and pieces from other goalkeepers, looking at how doing certain things helped them and, in turn, how that could help me. I was always striving to improve.

By the time I went to Stockport, I had already made my debut for Wolves. That was on August 23, 2005. I had not long turned 19. It was a Carling Cup tie at home to Chester. I remember not eating before the game – a far cry from sticking the Indian takeaway down my neck the night before my first match for Accrington. This time, I was proper nervous, playing for Wolves at Molineux and with a lot of top players in the team. We had Joleon Lescott, Mark Kennedy, Darren Anderton, Kenny Miller and more – some big names who I had trained with and who I knew had very high standards which I needed to follow.

I was never completely sure whether I was ready but I didn't have anything to worry about. We won 5-1 and, by the time Chester scored late in the game, it was all done and dusted. It was disappointing not to keen a clean sheet but I had made my Wolves debut and I was buzzing. Playing with those top players gave me the confidence that it was something I would be able to do again in the future. They made it easy for me. When you play with those players, they do everything that little bit better and easier and, in turn, that makes it more comfortable for the young, rookie goalkeeper.

Finally, I had broken through. Finally, I had played a first-team match for Wolves and I was absolutely delighted. By the time of the next round of the Carling Cup, at Watford, I had gone off to Stockport and still had many more loans to come. But before the next one, came two more appearances for Wolves. The first was in the Carling Cup, again at the start of a season, at Chesterfield. I don't remember much of the game if I'm being honest, although as it finished 0-0, that's probably no surprise. It went to a penalty shoot-out which we lost 6-5.

I was then back in action for Wolves just three days later, at Molineux against Luton. It wasn't quite normal circumstances, though, because I went on after 87 minutes. Matt Murray was back in goal but went down injured near the end of the game. Despite my short contribution, It was quite a baptism given it was my League debut in an important game and we were protecting a 1-0 lead. There were nearly 20,000 inside Molineux, by far the biggest crowd I had played in front of at that time. It feels like you are on to a hiding to nothing going on so late as a keeper when you are 1-0 up. If you make a save or two, people expect it but, if you let one in, you can end up getting the blame.

It's a horrible situation and I was desperate not to do anything which would cost us the three points. Again, the nervous tension was there and my mind started going overtime but I felt a lot calmer and more confident than I had before. I actually found myself with a fair bit to do as Luton pushed forward for an equaliser. Two wicked corners were sent into the near post and I remember coming for one, climbing over a few players and getting the ball after a bit of a scramble. It was just like that Academy game against Birmingham all those years before!

So I managed a few touches and achieved a psychological breakthrough in making a winning League debut for Wolves on top of the cup games for them and the loan appearances elsewhere. It was a big thing for me at the time to have played in the Championship for Wolves. It was all about stepping stones.....my debut at Accrington, my debut in the cup for Wolves and then that League debut at a considerably higher level. It was about experiencing it, getting it in the bag and then moving on to the next challenge.

Perhaps there was the feeling at the time that I wasn't moving quickly enough in terms of opportunities and pushing towards that sustained breakthrough at Molineux. But, when I looked back at the age of 26 or 27, at all the loans and clubs I had been to, I realised I had been very fortunate to get such a good grounding. Goalkeepers generally reach the first team a bit later than outfield players, so all those opportunities I was given were a positive. It all helped with building up to where I wanted to be; in the number one shirt at Wolves and maybe, just maybe, one day, representing Nigeria.

9

A new arrival

If reaching where I wanted to be in football was going to be a long haul, then that was exactly the same with my leukaemia diagnosis. As soon as I had received advice and taken that decision to be treated at Christie's, I quickly came to terms with it all and accepted what I needed to do to recover. And once I had got myself to Manchester, I was really keen for the chemotherapy to start.

Everything had to be completely right before I could begin and I remember it being delayed and me having to wait. Then I had my first injection and we were off and running. At the time I didn't know anything about chemotherapy. My pre-conception was that I was going to have to go into a special room with people in masks sorting out the treatment. As the nurse inserted the cannula, and I could feel the cold sensations going through my veins, it was a strange feeling to know that this injection was toxic and was going to make me feel sick, but was also what was going to help to save my life.

So I think it was natural, when starting treatment, to be waiting for something really bad to happen and to start feeling unwell. But, in that first month, it wasn't too bad. I felt a bit ill over one or two days and was sometimes tired but the main thing which showed was a loss of weight. I remember starting at around 98kg and, by the end of the month, losing 10kg and being down to 88kg.

As I have mentioned, I was keen to do whatever I could to help myself with those parts I could control and that included food. After a lot of research, I had decided to go Vegan. Saba and I started to read a lot of books about Dr Sebi, which talked about feeding the body the right nutrients which come from herbs and vegetables. I would try and get as many nutrients into my body as possible from drinking smoothies that were full of kale, turmeric and other herbs. Saba was cooking meals for me at home that my family and friends would bring in.

We knew that my body was going to be receiving a lot of toxins from the treatment, so we wanted to do whatever we could to give my body some fuel, but also a rest from animal products and grains that were difficult to digest.

I also went for walks whenever I could and was determined to keep myself busy when I was well enough When you stay in bed a lot, your muscles can waste away, so I would try and get outside whenever I could. It was still summer, so that helped.

My exercise would depend on how my bloods were doing with the treatment and there were places I needed to keep away from, particularly where there were lots of people and a risk of infection. I would go for a walk down the road towards Didsbury and stop and read a book. I'd be sat on a bench or someone's garden wall reading and it is amazing what you appreciate when you are in that situation. The fresh air, the light, all the things you take for granted suddenly become a real highlight. It eventually reached a point where I couldn't go out because I was neutropenic. I had a low level of white blood cells which meant I had a really high risk of infection. I had to stay in my room but had an exercise bike brought up from Wolves, so I could still do a bit of spin work when I felt up to it.

But the number of visitors had to be reduced and if anyone had even a slight cough, they weren't allowed to come because my immune system was so low. It was during this time that my little girl was born. Mila now had a baby sister, Maya. I had been at Christie's around a week when she came along and I know Saba had been desperate for the birth to come because she wanted to be able to support me in Manchester as soon as possible. So it was never going to be a straightforward and magical birth like so many are. It was so strange thinking about the birth of my second daughter and to know I wasn't going to be there. I knew Saba was in labour, her friend Michelle was keeping me up to date and then she got them both on Facetime after Maya arrived.

It is still so difficult to describe my feelings. I knew how fantastic it all was but I wasn't there to properly share in all the emotion. I wanted to have that connection with my new daughter but it wasn't there yet and that just didn't feel right. And all this just a few weeks after I thought my life was fine and we were really looking forward to Maya's arrival and to sharing it together. So much was going around my head and it was a surreal mix of happiness and at the same time not being elated or on cloud nine because I hadn't been there at the birth.

My mum and my sister Tayla were in Manchester at the time and I remember

Mum telling me she just knew Maya had arrived. They had gone out for a walk and stumbled on a church with the door open and asked the vicar if they could go in. Mum has never been a religious person, she believes in what she believes, but it just felt right for her to go in that day, to have some peace and quiet, because she wasn't in a very good place with everything I was going through. She said a prayer for me and by the time they got back to the hospital, I was able to pass on the message that Maya had been born.

It was about a week later than I finally saw her as Saba brought the girls up to the hospital. Babies were not usually allowed where I was but we were given special dispensation and at last I had the chance to hold her. That made such a huge difference. It felt like she was mine then, my daughter, and not just this baby I had seen on a photo or a video clip. I could see that she looked like me and we started to have that connection between father and daughter. We had a photo taken of the four of us and it was so nice to have the family up there. Meeting Maya for the first time gave me that extra motivation to get through it all.

It was great to see Mila again as well, and being with Saba and our two beautiful girls was just what I needed. Despite the circumstances, I truly felt blessed to have them. At this time Mila was four and obviously we hadn't told her the seriousness of what I was battling against. Saba had explained to her that Daddy was in hospital and that she wouldnt be able to see me every day like when we were at home. Mila provided a lot of light relief when she came up. She was at that age when life was all about exploring. She would come into the room and be like: 'What is this?' and 'What does this do?' The electric bed would be going all over the shop as she pressed the different buttons, then it would be onto the television and trying to get Minions on. She knew I was unwell but not the extent of it, and all of this was a trip into the unknown.

I genuinely believe Maya arrived into our lives, and our family, for a reason. That's because Saba shouldn't really have become pregnant. She was using the contraceptive coil at the time and I remember when she started experiencing sickness and some of those early pregnancy signs. We were in London and she just couldn't believe she could be pregnant. She bought a test and it turned out that she was. Then we were a bit worried about whether the baby would be okay, as the coil had been misplaced.

As soon as we got over the shock of it all, we were all very excited, most of all Mila, as she was preparing to be a big sister! We read afterwards there was a two per cent chance Saba might get pregnant, so it was just another amazing feature of our lives over the last few years.

Saba also experienced a spiritual awakening during the birth, which she still finds difficult to describe even to this day. During the birth she felt like she was in a different dimension, and almost a meditative state. She kept seeing circles which she interprets as the circle of life. After the birth Saba then felt a calming sense, which convinced her that our family was going to be fine through this really tough period.

In terms of the pregnancy, the birth, and Maya being born so soon after I was diagnosed, she is a special little girl in so many different ways. Although she wasn't planned, we were still buzzing and so happy she was on her way. And that, with all those circumstances, is why I think she is here for a reason.

I had to go to a sperm bank around the time of starting my treatment. I had already had my bone marrow done, which, as anyone who has had that procedure knows, is very strange. You have a hole drilled in your back near your pelvis to get your bone marrow and, while I'm not sure what the science is, it can test for the disease and work out what level it is at. Only problem is, my bone is very hard, which made the process even more tricky.

The sperm bank visit is a funny enough experience at a normal time and is even more surreal when your life is under threat. I had to fill out a load of forms and answer question after question, all while I was still shell-shocked following my diagnosis. Of course it was for a very important reason – to freeze my sperm in case we decided to have more kids because there was a chance the leukaemia treatment would leave me infertile. It was just another mad time for me, sitting there and wondering what on earth my life had turned into. I was given a pot and a private room and remember having a bit of a giggle to be honest. It felt like something from an American Pie film and I recall checking the couch to see if there were any stains there (sorry, folks!). There weren't any magazines around or anything and I was just left to get on with it; another strange experience at a time when I was on such an emotional rollercoaster.

There was so much of that going on in terms of trying to adapt to this huge change in my life. In those first few weeks of treatment, I had a lot of time to think, especially at night. The ward was silent, unlike the usual business of the day, and I would be tossing and turning to get comfortable. I'd be thinking about Saba and Mila, then Maya after she came along. At times, it got very lonely, with just me and my thoughts. That is where that mental strength had to come in again.

I had to use that to tell myself to shut up with any negative thoughts and keep concentrating on what I needed to do to get better. My mind was something I had to try to control, and with all the thoughts going through my head it was like I had a peaceful security guarding my mind and my thoughts. If I started to think: 'What will my family do without me?', my guard would step in. 'I accept those thoughts but there is no place for you in here.'

I was being checked every four hours at the hospital, so it was difficult to get any proper sleep. Trusting in the process, that was the key. And that was what would really help me in the months which followed. After evaluating everything in those early days and weeks, I decided that trusting the process was the best way. I didn't know too much about how I would react to the treatment, or what exactly was going to be coming my way in terms of side effects. But I had to trust in the process and trust in those people who had my life in their hands.

I was still getting fabulous support from people from so many different sources. Wolves fans, in particular, were doing so much to support me and raise awareness and funds for the Cure Leukaemia charity, including a 24-hour penalty shoot-out at the stadium organised by one of those supporters, Steve Plant. I had been asked by the Wolves press office to send a video message which my mum filmed and they played on the big screens before the first game of the season against Middlesbrough the next day. Mum, Saba and the kids went to the game and Mila walked out with the teams. There was also a big mosaic in the South Bank behind the goal where, in other circumstances, I might have been taking my place at the start of the season.

I remember watching Mila walk out and receiving pictures that had me welling up with emotion in my bed. The innocence of my beautiful Mila walking out, mixed with the show of love I had received, really had taken me aback. I was lying in bed looking at the screen and feeling so proud looking at Mila, but also crushed that she didn't know why all this love and support was being shown to her father. There was that little bit of pressure as well, because everyone knows how mentally strong I am. All the talk and encouragement underlined that they expected me to beat this thing. But what would happen if my body couldn't handle it? If my body wasn't able to fight the leukaemia? If that happened, there was nothing I could do. I'd be gone. So there was this feeling of pressure about what would happen if I couldn't get better? And how hard it was going to be even if I did.

One person who knew all about that is Joe Thompson, another footballer, who

I saw quite early in the process. Joe was pretty much on his way out of treatment at Christie's as I was on my way in. He has twice been diagnosed with Hodgkin Lymphoma, which twice affected his career, but more importantly twice he has lived to tell the tale. I didn't know Joe before we met there but we had mutual friends and he was at Christie's for a check-up when I bumped into him. I had a good chat with him about what he had been through to see what was in store and I know he had an even longer chat with my mum as well. That was important for her as she had a lot of questions which she wanted answered and Joe was massively helpful in that respect. Mum was nervous at the time. She wanted to know what was going to happen to her son along with the unanswerable question: Why? Joe was another person I got on well with and could get information from. Having come through cancer twice, he was another positive example for me to focus on. He provided another marker and is someone I have stayed in really close touch with and am sure I will continue to do so.

The start of the 2017/18 football season brought really mixed feelings. I felt I should still be out there playing for Wolves, but here I was in hospital with a really tough few months ahead. It was still a relief, though, in as much as it gave me something to do and to watch. Wolves sorted me out with a live stream to watch all the games and that was a really nice distraction, apart from the odd game like Sheffield United away when I was so pissed off after Conor Coady was sent off that I switched it straight off. In doing so, I missed the two goals scored by my mate Leon Clarke. Sorry, Leon! Whether I was in my room at hospital or the apartment in Manchester, it was good to be able to watch the games and keep in touch with how the lads were doing, which was pretty well. They weren't really missing me too much, were they?

That first bout of treatment went on for a month or so. A few weeks after that, I settled into the apartment in Manchester and Maya had come along. It was all fairly steady. I had lost weight but wasn't feeling too bad and everyone was happy with how the first phase was going. I suffered some nausea and was tired and in bed more than normal. But overall, I didn't feel too different.

I am not sure you can ever completely know what is going to happen with treatment for such a serious illness but those initial chemotherapy sessions were a walk in the park compared with what was to come. After those first four weeks, my blood results were good, which gave me a boost, and also prompted the doctor to say on the Friday that there was no need to wait before starting the next phase. A break between treatments is sometimes allowed but I didn't really want any gaps, so that was good news to send me back to Birmingham with for the weekend. I was still in the process of completing the move to the apartment in Manchester and wanted to crack on with everything, so getting back there on the Monday morning was a good sign. The way I saw it was that if the treatment was going to last around eight months, the more we could get done quickly, the sooner I could be home.

The next phase of treatment was more intense than the first. This meant receiving some form of chemotherapy every day as well as intravenous treatment every couple of weeks and four injections a week. I was on tablets as well and started to feel considerably weaker. I remember, at the end of the first week, it had been a long day and I had seen the doctor before heading off at around 5pm. I had a couple of days break, so Dad was there and was going to drive me back to Birmingham. But we had only just started when I asked him to pull up. "I don't think I can do this journey today," I told him. I stayed in Manchester over the weekend, tried to relax and get some food inside me. But the treatment was starting to really hit me.

I also started getting some bleeding out of my backside, which was another potential side-effect of the chemotherapy. It meant I had to go back to Christie's for a couple of nights to make sure everything was fine and I could carry on with the treatment. My haemoglobin was getting low and platelets were starting to drop. I was starting to really suffer with fatigue. On another occasion when I was due to go back into Christie's, I remember getting my stuff together and nearly passing out. I was getting hot and sweaty and things were very tough. Even just the energy needed to put my belongings in a bag was starting to take so much effort. There is a lovely Scouse nurse at the hospital called Steph and she took one look at me and said: "You don't look too good, you know." She took my bag off me and sat me down before I was given the first of many blood transfusions I needed during the process.

That was another new development, one which took a bit of time for me to get my head around. Obviously, they tell you at the start of the treatment that you are likely to feel weak and will probably need blood and platelet transfusions. You listen but it is difficult to take it all in and imagine or visualise what it will be like when it happens. It is that unknown. How was I going to feel? How bad did it have to be to need a blood transfusion? What was it going to be like? Everything was explained to me properly but until I experienced it, I was never quite sure about the whole process. It is a mad feeling the first time someone else's blood is being pumped into you. But it was very much appreciated and just goes to show how important it is for people to donate blood. It certainly made me feel a whole lot better.

I was in the apartment during this second phase of treatment but was really struggling to look after myself by now. I wanted good, healthy food to keep my strength up as much as possible but even that was proving an ordeal. I would end up making soup or other meals that were easy to prepare. I was also spending a lot more time in hospital than during the earlier treatment. Although I didn't necessarily have to stay in for the chemotherapy, a blood or platelets transfusion took a few hours. So some days I'd arrive at Christie's at 10am and not leave until 10pm. There was always the opportunity to stay in overnight if needed but the staff would let me go back to the apartment if I wanted to.

Often, they asked if someone would be there and I occasionally lied and said 'yes' because I really wanted to get back there for the night. Unless I was feeling really sick, they were happy for me to go. I had breathing space in the apartment, although I was only doing the same as at the hospital and lying on the bed. It was quiet, my own space, and I didn't have to put a front on with anyone. I was quite particular about food as well and sometimes didn't eat all day in hospital as I wanted my own food back home. If I had the energy to make it, that is.

Most of the time, I had someone there to help. There was never a shortage of willing volunteers. Saba was looking after the kids back in Birmingham during the week because we had decided we didn't want Mila's life to change too much and we wanted to keep everything as normal as possible for her. She had started school, which was another really tough day for me. Missing her first day was devastating and I couldn't help but feel guilty about it. I had to reassure myself that I was missing this one to be there for the rest of her schooldays. Mum and Dad came up regularly to help me, my friends Robbie and Adam, and Sylvan Ebanks-Blake as well. They would bring food from Birmingham that Saba or my dad had set up and when it was an effort for me to buy ingredients or make dinner, they would help out. which was massive for me.

There were two particular times when I needed Mum's help. One night, when she was due to come next day, I phoned to ask where she was. She realised I was struggling because even without me saying I didn't need her, she got straight in the car. That's mums for you. She cooked me something but I was really bad then with diarrhoea and ended up going into hospital and being put on a drip. Another time, I was struggling when she visited towards the end of the second bout of treatment, and hadn't been eating. She went to Sainsbury's so she could cook me a meal but can remember me sniffing the food and looking ill. She apparently cried all the way home that night and although Tayla suggested they turned round again, she didn't think it would help me to see her so upset.

I suppose this was when I was looking like what people think of as a 'cancer patient' and it was so difficult for my loved ones. I looked forward to seeing Saba and the kids at the weekend but it was becoming hard for me to interact. We tried to have quality time but I would end up back in bed, trying to rest. I felt bad because Mila was so excited to see me and I also really wanted to bond with Maya and get to know her. I longed to help Saba with all the stresses that come with having a baby but, quite often, she took the kids out to give me some rest. It became an effort to get ready each morning, an effort to walk to the lift from the apartment and an effort to get from the reception to a taxi. I would often feel nauseous as the treatment took hold but wasn't really sick until six or seven months in when I had a bit of chocolate which came back very quickly!

I am not one who is generally nauseous and the way I was feeling, I often wanted to be sick to feel a bit better. So everything was starting to take its toll and I underwent four weeks of more aggressive treatment. At the end of it, I headed back to Birmingham for a few days' rest and take stock of where we were at. The plan was to return to Manchester on the Monday and see how my body had stood up to the treatment before deciding when I could go on to the next phase. How long to wait between treatments is dependent on many different factors and what the medical people think.

The first phase went straight into the second phase because I had been feeling okay and I'd always been keen to keep pushing on. But there was no way I'd ever have been able to fool the clinical staff. I couldn't put a front on or start jogging on the spot to prove I was feeling good. It wasn't like trying to convince a manager I was fit to play when that wasn't quite the truth. It was also dependent on the blood counts, which they would check to determine if I was ready. There was no way I'd be able to kid them. So it was back home to rest after a pretty intense time and then plan for returning to Christie's first thing Monday. But what is that phrase about the best-laid plans going awry? There was absolutely no chance I would be heading back as scheduled. Instead, I was entering what proved to be one of the scariest times of my life.

10

Promoted to the Prem

Talking of preparing, you can't really plan for much in football as it is always so unpredictable. Waiting was also something I had become accustomed to at Wolves, as I wondered when I might get an opportunity to show what I could do. I had been through a few loan spells and had learned bits from all of them but never really knew when I might get a decent first-team opportunity. It was in 2008/09 that I enjoyed my first proper run in the side.

My first League start came in the September in a home game against Bristol City as Wayne Hennessey, who was the first choice at the time, was suspended after being sent off at Preston the previous week. We were flying, having drawn one and then won six in a row in the Championship – so no pressure! About 24,000 were inside Molineux that day and there was quite an atmosphere around the game, so it was a bit different to going on in the last few minutes against Luton a couple of seasons earlier. I knew in the build-up that I would be playing and that gave me time to prepare. Bristol City had made a decent start and hadn't previously conceded an away goal in the League and there was a lot of hype around comments made by Michael McIndoe, who had been at Wolves before.

So I was feeling a little bit nervous, which was natural, but I also felt ready. This was the next stepping stone and a big game at that against a big club. I had shown I was able to do it during my loan spells but now I had to prove I could do it at Wolves. It was a proper summer's day, both sets of fans were going at it, and it was a really exciting game to be a part of. We had Kights (Michael Kightly) and Jarvo (Matt Jarvis) causing havoc on the wings and were so good going forward. Kights and Sylvan Ebanks-Blake got the goals as we won 2-0 and I felt I did well, going for a few crosses and making the right decisions when I needed to.

Coming off the pitch at Molineux in that incredible atmosphere after keeping a clean sheet on my full League debut for the club…I was on such a high. I was absolutely buzzing and am not sure there is anything better for a player than that feeling at the end of a game like that when it has all gone so well. It was the first time I had been able to taste that feeling at Wolves and to be 'in' the game in front of a big crowd.

The gaffer, Mick McCarthy, brought Wayne straight back for the next game against Reading, which was understandable given how well he had been doing and the fact we had made a great start to the season. But after we lost 3-0, our first League defeat of the campaign, he decided to give me another opportunity. He felt he had me and Wayne battling for the shirt and also potentially Matt Murray, who was coming back from injury. He said it was going to be a fair fight and that Wayne was just a bit deflated and jaded after the loss against Reading. It wasn't the best spell for the team straight after as we lost the next two away games, 3-1 at Swansea and 5-2 at Norwich, in between beating Coventry at home. But I was starting to feel a real part of things having got some games and was growing in confidence.

Mick was good to play for and I don't think I was ever on the end of one of his 'rockets'! In that Norwich game, I made a bad mistake which led to a goal but I played well apart from that despite the scoreline. Bizarrely, I can remember to this day that the warm-up before that game at Carrow Road was probably the best I had ever done. I didn't drop a single ball, I was razor-sharp and recall someone ripping one towards the top corner and I just plucked it out of the air. Then I go on and concede five. That's football! Right...on to the error. The game was still goalless just before the half-hour when a free-kick came in under the bar. Because of how confident I was feeling after that warm-up, I thought I could catch it. I didn't even want to tip it over and concede a corner. I just felt I'd be able to claim it and get us quickly up the pitch. Unfortunately, it didn't turn out like that. As I caught it, I went back over my own goal-line. Own goal Ikeme. Just a complete nightmare.

The next day, Mick asked how I thought I had done – "not very good" was my reply. He then told me he thought I had done well and that mistakes happen, that I needed to reflect on my overall game and that I had been brilliant. That gave me the confidence to take into the next game and made it easier to brush off the things I felt I hadn't done so well. Norwich has never been a great place for me, as was proved when I was sent off there a few years later to rule me out of the big FA Cup tie at Liverpool. But from that defeat in 2008, we went on and won seven games in a row and it was a great time for me.

Unfortunately, it wasn't destined to last and, on a bruising night at Sheffield United, even though we won 3-1, I was one of several players who finished with injuries. It was the same night that Matty Murray picked up a really bad injury playing on loan for Hereford, so it wasn't a good one for Wolves at all. I still have the scars from Bramall Lane! Someone studded me and the impact went right through my shin-pad, so I ended up with a hole in my shin. I also took an elbow in the oblique and abdomen area, and then, feeling a bit sore from all that, something just went when I kicked the ball and I had to be replaced just before half-time.

It was another season where I couldn't quite get fit and stay fit, which was so frustrating as I was going well and the team were flying. I felt comfortable in that Championship environment and I loved that game at Sheffield United in particular because of the hostile atmosphere. After that, though, my season was pretty much over as I continued to struggle with back problems. I was able to do most things in training but wasn't necessarily kicking the ball a great distance so the injury wouldn't surface. I got back in against Preston in the January but I wasn't completely right. At one point, I went out for a cross which I should have caught but I couldn't get there and they scored from it. It turned out that I had fractured my back in that game, which explained why I had been struggling with my movement. I could barely move at all after that and knew it was all over for the season.

I had made 13 appearances, my most in a season at that time, and, while I hadn't played a massive role, I felt I had contributed as the team went on to clinch the Championship title. I thought I had done well enough, kept some clean sheets and helped us win a fair few games. I would like to have been more heavily involved, as any player would, but I couldn't do anything about the injuries and Wayne was also a very good keeper to try and dislodge. I wasn't involved in any more games but I felt really proud of the part I played and still do.

It was another breakthrough for me at Wolves, knowing I could test myself at Championship level and proving I could do it. And the changing room was absolutely unbelievable and such a privilege to be involved with. The atmosphere among the squad was wicked, as good as I was a part of throughout my whole career. With Andy Keogh, Wardy (Stephen Ward), Kights, Sylvan, Stacky (Graham Stack) when he came in and so many more, it was just brilliant. So many of us were of similar ages and we all got on so well, and were also similar in terms of our hunger to be successful. A lot of us had either come through the Academy or through the lower leagues and were so driven and desperate to make a mark in the game. Even in the times when I was only in for treatment, I felt a real part of it all and we shared a lot of outside interests. If we managed to grab a night out, which may just have happened from time to time, everyone would be there.

Pre-seasons were always really hard work but we would all put the effort in and Mick would let us loose now and again for a night out where there would be so many laughs. None of us had kids then and no massive responsibilities, so life was fairly relaxed away from the football. It was such a good place to be and an incredible changing room to be around, which makes a big difference at a club. I am probably closest now to Sylvan, which is quite funny because it was certainly not always like that. Let's just say that we took some time to warm to each other! He is quite similar in personality to me, a bit stand-offish when he first meets someone. So we spent a while being stand-offish with each other after he arrived. He is one of my closest friends in football now but we didn't speak at all for months when he arrived in the January before our promotion season.

He would just sit in his seat in the dressing room, all fairly quiet, just keeping an eye on what was going on. That is how I was at times, sizing everyone up. For Sylvan, he was settling into a new club as well. Yet by the time the promotion-winning season came around, we had very much clicked and got on really well from there. A lot of us at the time were young and similar in our experiences but even the senior lads were top guys around the place. Jody Craddock was the one who had been at the top of the game for a long time and while he was a fairly quiet character, he'd have a giggle with us as well.

Everyone had so much respect for Jody. He didn't say a lot but, when he did, everyone would. And, a lot of the time, it was on the pitch where Jody did his talking. That was where he led by example. We all knew what he would give the team every single time he crossed the white line. He helped so many of the young lads and he'd be bang up for the Christmas parties despite the age difference. More often than not, he would turn up in some really mad fancy-dress outfit. That seemed to become his speciality. He'd get himself involved in the thick of it and we'd get to see a different side of him where he would be massively into all the banter.

Another experienced arrival later in the season was Graham Stack and wow,

Above: An early trip out with Dad. Right: So many happy family times growing up - even the thought of going to school!

Left: A hug with Mum.

Left: Relaxing with Dad - and apparently revealing a bit of an interest in trains.

Right: Yes I was a Villa fan growing up and used to love going to games with my dad.

A proud day, signing my first contract (above) with Mum and Dad and Wolves club secretary Richard Skirrow. Below: With my fellow scholars. Pictured from left are Keith Lowe, Luke Bradley, me, Kevin O'Connor, Jonny Steele, Richard Skirrow, Chris Evans, Michael Townsend, Matthew Barnes-Homer, Mark Goodhead and Tom Bonnar. Left: Training as a young pro.

Left: Proud as punch to be 'directing the traffic' from between the sticks at Compton. Below: I learned from many highly experienced team-mates, including Michael Oakes and Paul Jones.

Contrasting moods....deep in thought at training and a bit more animated after we won a penalty shoot-out against Aldershot. Below: Of my many loan spells, I really enjoyed working under Neil Warnock at QPR, where former Wolves skipper Keith Curle (tracksuited, left) was also on board.

Chilling in the dressing room before a cup tie against Aldershot (above) and feeling the long arm of the law (left) following a lively derby victory at Walsall.

That ‘champion’ feeling x 2. Above: Keepers’ union was strong as we won the 2008/09 Championship with Wayne Hennessey and me both involved. Below: Celebrations (some more over the top than others!) late in the win at Orient that ultimately clinched the League One title. Left: Sticking to the collective hard-work ethic that brought us our success.

Top: Sky TV duties with my good mate Sylvan after a battling victory at Blackpool during Stale Solbakken's reign. Lower photos: Give me some weights and I am content enough....running is okay, the hard yards have to be put in as well, but......

he added something completely different. I'd go as far as to say he was completely off the scale. Anybody who has met or knows Stacky knows exactly what they are going to get from him. Without doubt, he is one of the funniest men I have met in football. There were a few moaners about as well, which you get in every dressing room. Neill Collins could be an absolute nightmare but I mean that in a nice way. He was on everyone's case all the time and probably pissed me off a fair few times, but he would leave everything on the pitch in support of his team-mates. Then there was Karl Henry. The captain. How he loved a debate and an argument! He still does. If you told Karl the sky was blue, he would argue that it wasn't. There were times when I felt I wanted to argue a point but it really wasn't worth it and I would walk off rather than spend all day talking about it. Karl was just so competitive and when the table tennis table came out, you just knew he would spend hours practising on it before taking the lads on.

Although a lot of us were young, we had such a strong competitive edge and a competitive toughness. We were close and would dig each other out if the time was right. There were a lot of big characters in that dressing room. It was the right combination at the right time and, looking back, I can see just how strong in character every single one of those players were. I am sure that mindset was something Mick thought about when he was building the squad. We could handle ourselves in games as well and, despite the low average age, this was not a Wolves team which would ever be bullied.

Neilly, Jody – they wouldn't give the opposition strikers a minute – Stears (Richard Stearman) too. And he had a bit of finesse about him. Karl could look after himself on the pitch as well and I don't think he was ever properly appreciated for the role he carried out for Wolves. On the pitch, we all appreciated what he could do, that was for sure. I know he overstepped the mark sometimes but that was because he was always prepared to go in for that challenge or go after someone who had laid it on one of the lads.

Wayne, Foles (Kevin Foley), Jarvo, Dave Edwards, David Jones....again, they were young but also so mentally strong. When you put all that together – the mix of speed, ability and mental toughness, I don't think it is any surprise that we won the title in some style. And, at the top of it all, we had Mick, TC (Terry Connor) and a fantastic backroom staff. They created an environment where people were willing to run through brick walls for each other. Mick would accept mistakes from players but he would never accept not trying, so you always knew where you stood. He was always completely straight with everyone in that respect and he could be hard from time to time, but he was definitely a player's manager. You probably never got as close to him as you did to TC but he was the gaffer and we all had the ultimate respect for him. TC also wanted and demanded a high level of hard work from everyone but he was the one who might give you a bit of love when you needed it. He knew how to press the right buttons with players but, as well as an arm around the shoulder, he wouldn't hesitate to give you a rocket when you needed it.

Everything came together so well on and off the pitch and we had such an energy about us as a result. Kites and Jarvo were flying, Sylv, Lumes (Chris Iwelumo), Keogh and Vokesey (Sam Vokes) were banging the goals in and we had so much quality all over the pitch. With our desire to push forward and attack, we didn't necessarily keep a lot of clean sheets but we would always back ourselves to out-score teams at that level. We had electric pace, which is so important, and felt so confident going into every game – the exuberance of youth, I suppose.

Ultimately, I guess we all believed together and in everything we were doing. Mick, TC, the staff, the players, the club – everyone worked so hard for themselves and for each other. As a squad, it worked on the pitch and it worked off the pitch and we made sure we celebrated what was a fantastic achievement at the end of a long, hard season. After all, we had just been promoted to the Premier League!

11

"Ride it out, son"

It was while watching Super Sunday and the Premier League back in Birmingham that things really started to deteriorate. I was home for a few days having spent a month in Manchester on the second phase of treatment, and my mate Robbie had come around to watch the football. Around 6pm, I wasn't feeling right. Not right at all. I had a headache and said I needed to go to sleep, so I went upstairs to bed.

My temperature was a bit high and I remember getting to sleep but when I woke up a few hours later, it had shot up to 38 degrees. I was proper sweating, feeling really weak and disorientated and had no idea what to do. Should I try and get to Manchester? Go into hospital in Birmingham? What was for the best? Every time we checked my temperature, it had gone up, so I rang Christie's and told them what was happening. They arranged for an ambulance to come straight round, then checked my blood pressure and temperature before taking me under the blue lights to Good Hope Hospital in Sutton Coldfield. I remember walking out of the house, thinking I could fall over at any time. I was so hot, it was difficult to explain, weak, shivery and just not with it at all. They started getting fluids inside me at the hospital and tried to take some blood.

Saba's Mum had gone around to look after the kids, so my mum and Saba were able to come and see me. I'm just glad, even now, that Mila was in bed at home and hadn't seen the state I was in. I really didn't want her to see me like I was. That was one rough night, I have to say.

I was getting fluids inside me but couldn't stop shaking and felt so cold. Yet the nurse wouldn't give me a blanket because my temperature was so high. We tried to contact my consultant Manos to let him know I was in A & E and to tell the Heartlands Hospital. Among all the physical issues, I was also worrying about what on earth was going on and what exactly was happening to me. I had just come through a really intense spell of chemotherapy and already I had caught something. All I was thinking was that I had to make sure I didn't catch anything else while I was in hospital. I didn't want the situation to get even worse.

I just couldn't sleep, still shivering, and had a really uncomfortable night before being transferred in an ambulance from Good Hope to Heartlands the next day. I was put on a ward there but still couldn't stop shaking. My body was physically jolting and soon it had been going on for 24 hours. My temperature was sky-high and showing no sign of falling and I wasn't eating anything, just drinking what I could. In the depths of everything, I just curled up into a ball on the bed, saying to myself in my head: 'Keep riding it, son, keep riding it'.

That is all I could think about, to keep riding it out, and hoping it would pass. I had never felt so bad in my life. Then I started to hallucinate. Every time I shut my eyes, I saw images of dead and dismembered bodies, piles of bodies on the floor. It was like a horror movie every time I closed my eyes, pure evil, which had me questioning my sanity and, in turn, was not letting me sleep. I would literally have to pass out from exhaustion even to get a few hours.

I was having all sorts of tests and, by the third day, I remember someone from Intensive Care coming to look at me. It didn't click until afterwards and maybe I just thought they were doing the rounds or having a look around the wards. But then I clocked it. They were there to see if I needed to go into ICU (the intensive care unit). During the nights, I couldn't stop shaking and even when they were pumping fluids into me, it wasn't having any effect. One of the nurses came in on one of the nights, sat by the bed and asked if she could say a prayer with me. It certainly felt like I needed divine intervention.

I was getting really dehydrated and started to suffer from diarrhoea as well. They were still doing scans, including a CT scan, and I didn't want to see anyone other than Saba. I couldn't face anyone else. I wasn't even looking at my phone or taking interest in anything. 'Keep riding it, son'. That was all that kept me going. Saba knew what was going on and how I was and would relay that back to the family. During the night, she would call the ward or Manos to see if there had been any change. She must have been terrified seeing me the way I was. She said she had ever seen anybody shiver like that. It was more like rocking. And it felt like I wasn't getting any better.

Manos was constantly coming in to check on me and updating us but you could tell he was a bit nervous and not his bubbly self. I knew he was worried and he told us there was a possibility that whatever was wrong could cause problems with my heart. So I had to have a camera down my throat to see what was going on – I had been through a lot of procedures during my treatment and another one didn't bother me much.

I went into the room and they explained what was going to happen. I was so weak, having not eaten properly for four days as I just couldn't stomach anything. But if before I thought I'd be okay with another procedure, I was very quickly put in my place. The camera going down, with everything that I had been struggling with, was probably the worst experience of my life. I felt I couldn't breathe, that I was choking and gasping for air. The doctor had said that if I wanted to stop at any time, I just needed to tap him. I have never, ever quit on anything in my life. Anyone who knows me will tell you, I don't quit. Simple as that. It's just not me. But, feeling as weak as I was and barely able to breathe, I was so, so close to tapping him. To make it stop. So close. That feeling is still with me, even now.

Again, it was my mind that saved me. Despite all those thoughts of being able to stop the pain, my mind just kept saying: 'Don't tap out, don't tap out'. Even at my very lowest, I was determined. If I had stopped, we might have lost out on a chance to find out what was going on and what it was that was making me so ill. The procedure must have gone on for 10-15 minutes but it felt like a whole lot longer. The camera went down further and further and feeling it inside me was strange. It felt like there was no room inside me for it to go further. I was sweating, gasping, trying to be sick, all at the same time. As soon as it started going down, I had started to sweat and have never sweated as much in my life. I was dripping.

I knew Saba was supposed to be coming to the hospital and, half-way through the process, recall thinking: 'I really hope she is not outside the room, waiting'. She would have heard all of this going on and me struggling, trying to be sick. As it turned out, she was there waiting and had heard everything. When I went out, I caught her eye as she looked at me. She looked totally horrified by what she saw. I was washed out anyway with no energy and now I was dripping with sweat and feeling completely disorientated. Feeling and looking so weak, sitting in a wheelchair, then knowing she had been listening and knowing I couldn't hide how I was feeling this time.....sadly, it was pretty obvious. Saba said later she had been sitting outside the whole time and had actually gone up to the desk and asked if it was normal to hear those awful sounds coming from the room.

I was pushed back to my room in the wheelchair and remember getting back on to my bed and falling asleep, totally and utterly exhausted. I was still feeling absolutely dreadful but at least that bit was over. When I look back, this was undoubtedly one of the worst points of my recovery. That test was such a rough procedure to have at any time, let alone when I was feeling so ill with everything my body was going through. But it needed to be done, we needed to find out what was wrong. And I gradually started to feel slightly better. Slowly but surely, I had a bit more energy and everything came back to me a little.

Maybe it was the fluids and the drugs starting to take effect, maybe I was on the road to recovery from whatever it was. Or maybe not. I remember waking up one morning, the first day I had a bit of energy, and looking at my phone. I hadn't checked it since going into hospital on the Sunday. I hadn't been capable and hadn't wanted to. But when I did check my messages, I noticed the screen was all blurred. Initially, I thought it had broken but how could it have been? I hadn't touched it in four or five days and it was fine when I had been admitted.

The nurse came into the room and I asked her if the phone was broken. Her reply? 'No, it's fine'. Not necessarily what I wanted to hear and then, when I tried to look at the toilet sign, I couldn't even see that properly. When you look around a hospital room, there isn't much there to take your interest or fix your eyes on. But it was definite. I couldn't focus properly on my phone, nor on the sign. It started to dawn on me that something else had come along, another serious setback off the back of a few days of agony.

It was difficult to imagine things getting even the slightest bit worse but, oh yes, that is what had happened. My eyesight had disappeared. Everything was just a blur. All this after everything else that had gone on over a few months. As I continued to try and deal with everything that was being thrown at me, now I couldn't even see.

12

A loan Wolf

In contrast, the path was there to see for all connected with Wolves during the summer of 2009. All roads led to the Premier League. Having played a bit-part as we had won promotion and the Championship, I was looking forward to trying to stake a claim to be involved.

We went to Australia for the pre-season, which was tough fitness-wise but a great experience, although Mick McCarthy had brought in Marcus Hahnemann to add to the goalkeeping department. Matt Murray was on his way back from injury, so that left Wayne Hennessey, myself and Buddy (Hahnemann) to fight it out. Wayne had finished the previous season well and Marcus was the new signing, so it was likely I was going to be the one struggling to be involved. I remember looking at Marcus and thinking he was a good keeper and he played well at Wolves when he got in. But I felt I could match him. Although I was inexperienced compared with him, I thought I was in front of him in training and felt ready to go. So it was disappointing when I found myself third in the pecking order.

In the first couple of months, I was only even on the bench twice, for the Carling Cup ties with Swindon and Manchester United, so I knew it wouldn't be long before I was packing my bags and off on my travels again. I needed to play and, at the end of October, there was an opportunity to go to Charlton on a 28-day emergency loan. They had lost their main keeper Rob Elliot to injury and were in League One, so it was a good chance to get some games even if the first one took me back to Carlisle, where I had been part of a Stockport team beaten 6-0.

I don't know what it was about Carlisle and fortunately I would have better memories of playing against them later for Wolves but Charlton lost that day, too. They also went out to Southampton in the Johnstone's Paints Trophy but I was in goal for a couple of big wins against MK Dons and Bristol Rovers and a draw against Yeovil. Darren Randolph was the substitute keeper and it was a good month, which I enjoyed. But when Rob returned to fitness, it wasn't long before I was back at Wolves.

Pretty soon, I was on the move again, though, this time to Sheffield United. They are a very big club and it was another great opportunity for me, working under Kevin Blackwell and in the Championship. Unfortunately, it proved extremely short-lived; even shorter than the month which a lot of emergency loans last. We won 3-2 at Bristol City in a dramatic game which included them equalising in the last minute and Darius Henderson then grabbing a winner, and followed up with another tough win, 1-0 at Plymouth. But I pulled my calf in that game with about 15 minutes remaining and there was no keeper on the bench. I had to see it out and spent the last quarter of an hour praying the ball didn't come near me.

As it turned out, another late goal, from James Harper, was enough, so although it was a big disappointment to have to return to Wolves injured, at least I did so off the back of two wins out of two for such a big club. My next port of call was QPR just over a month later and this time for a good few months – long enough to really establish myself in the team.

It was a bit mad there at the time, with Formula One bosses Bernie Ecclestone and Flavio Briatore in charge. It was all fairly hectic. I had a sign of things to come when Paul Hart signed me on loan and his time as manager ended before I had even played a game. It was maybe four or five days into my stay there that he was sent on his way but, in football, you have to get on with things, so that's what I did. Mick Harford was put in temporary charge, with former keeper Tony Coton as his assistant. Mick was a man's man, no-nonsense, and I have always found that I like people of that nature. He was good to work for, as was the goalkeeping coach David Rouse, and that was a great learning curve for me.

Still though, nobody could escape the fact that QPR were in a mess and struggling. The changing room was all over the place. There was absolutely no cohesion around the club. The owners were constantly coming in before and after games, asking the players what the manager was doing and why he was making certain decisions. That is never productive and made for a very strange atmosphere with no-one really knowing who they could trust. I will say one thing, though – the food at the training ground was absolutely amazing! There was an Italian chef in the canteen and it was like a five-star menu for the players every day. Sadly, the football didn't live up to it.

So despite Mick being a good man-manager, it was no surprise that results weren't great and also no surprise that the owners soon decided to appoint a new face. Step forward Neil Warnock. He turned the place around. This was March, 2010, and he was already the fifth manager in charge at QPR during the one season but he got things going with a couple of quick wins, the first against Albion. I remember the day Warnock arrived. We trained for an hour, no longer, and he told us that if we had a niggle, don't bother going out, just stay in the gym. Training was tough, another shin-pads job like with Mick McCarthy but, if any player was feeling even ten per cent below par for whatever reason, then Warnock didn't want to risk them being out there.

He got us moving right from the off, with a fresh intensity that transferred on to the pitch. I got on well with him and it was just a shame I had to leave about ten games into his time because I had reached the maximum days allowed for the three-month emergency loan. He knew how to get a changing room going and I would love to have worked with him for longer. He knew how to get players' confidence levels up but also paid attention to the details off the pitch, which always help keep a dressing room positive.

International breaks were a good example. Two weeks before, he would tell any players that weren't going away with their countries that they would be in on the Thursday morning and then off Friday, Saturday, Sunday and Monday. He'd tell us that if we wanted to book flights and get away for a few days, we could do it. It might sound fairly small but players love being told that in advance. It was a carrot dangled in front of you and something to look forward to providing you took care of business in training and on the pitch. I also remember Warnock asking me: 'Why the hell aren't you playing at Wolves?' Even hearing that gave me a boost and he is one of the best at knowing just how to get the very most out of his players.

Adel Taarabt is one who has probably caused a lot of managers some problems. But, again, Warnock knew just how to treat him to get the best out of him and he did really well at QPR working under him. I loved my time there, played almost 20 games and proved to myself once again that I could succeed in the Championship. Unfortunately, my last appearance was a convincing defeat against Leicester but we'd had a decent run up to then. And, ironically, Leicester was my next destination.

In the pre-season before the 2010/11 campaign, I had a lot of minutes at Wolves but was quickly back down to third in the pecking order behind Wayne and Marcus. So I was waiting for a club to lose a keeper to injury, which happened at Leicester, so off I went to the East Midlands. It was a move I was really looking forward to, another big club and the location was good, meaning I could stay at home and just have a longer drive than from Castle Bromwich into Wolves. Having said that, it didn't work out as well as I had hoped.

Paulo Sousa was the manager and I remember going into training feeling really sharp. Then we went into the changing room before what I thought was going to be my first game and Conrad Logan's shirt was hanging up. Paulo pulled me and said that I had looked good in training but that I wasn't playing in the game. I wasn't best pleased. I could fight to be on the bench at Wolves. There was no point going to sit on the bench elsewhere.

I did manage to get in but my form stuttered a fair bit from there and I did my ankle the one Friday when we working on set-pieces for the following day's game. Then I did something to my shoulder, not a complete dislocation but it was painful enough. Leicester replaced Sousa with Sven Goran Eriksson and extended the loan because they wanted to keep me. But, when I tried to train, I was struggling with the shoulder. Each time I stretched, I felt a really sharp pain and eventually I went back to Wolves and ended up having the shoulder pinned. Not great! Not great at all. And that was it for me for that season, which meant another frustrating time.

Come the following pre-season, Marcus had moved on but Dorus De Vries had been brought in to battle with Wayne Hennessey and this time I knew I was going to be on my way out fairly early. Mick McCarthy always made sure everyone knew where they stood well in advance of the start of the season and he told me they would be looking to send me out on loan again. Middlesbrough came in and, while I remember thinking it was a long way away, again I knew the potential and size of the club and what valuable experience it was going to provide. Tony Mowbray was the manager and although they had two or three good keepers on the books, I was straight in from the start of the season.

Stephen Pears was the goalkeeping coach and everything backed up what I had been thinking in terms of Boro being a really good club. They made a great start and I remember once again learning off all the different coaches. Pearsy was a bit different. He was one of those coaches that would talk to you a lot and that is the approach I always preferred. He would do some training work, then stop and talk to me about goalkeeping. That meant I was picking up new information all the time.

I kept six clean sheets in ten games as Boro made a flying start, then suffered a hand injury. Something always seemed to happen when things were going well! At same time, their regular keeper Jason Steele had pretty much recovered from injury, so the timing was right for me to go back to Wolves. Doing so well during the loan also did me a big favour in terms of my contract situation. I had a year left at Wolves but, all of a sudden, I was in a far better negotiating position and you need that when you are going into discussions with Jez Moxey! In all seriousness, I always got on well with the chief executive. He was very clever and knew what he was doing, but was also very honest and we both always knew where we stood.

I still wasn't in the frame at Wolves but at least the club wanting to keep me gave me hope for the future. And the opportunity arose for me to go out and get even more game time with a loan at Doncaster. Jez wouldn't let me go until my future was secured and I had signed the new deal. But once that happened, I was off again for another switch to the Championship. Dean Saunders was in charge there and it's fair to say it wasn't the most organised club I have played for. Other loan players would come in just on the Friday to train, then play on the Saturday and disappear again. One of the players in that bracket was from Villa and lived in Birmingham. There was I, sitting in a bed and breakfast in Doncaster all week and wondering what exactly was going on.

There was a divide in the changing room and Dean was trying to juggle everything but it was always going to be difficult in those circumstances. I wasn't surprised when they finished up bottom of the Championship, 12 points adrift of safety. On a personal note, it did give me another 15 appearances, in which I continued to give my best and pick up more valuable experience. With the Boro loan, my total of 26 games was my best so far in one season and the Doncaster move only came to an end towards the end of the campaign because I was called back to Wolves after Wayne picked up a cruciate injury.

From there, I managed to get my one and only appearance in the Premier League, on the final day of the season at Wigan. I had been deputising for Dorus De Vries but he picked up an injury and I was sent on early in the second half. It wasn't the most positive of top-flight debuts. Wolves had already been relegated and TC (Terry Connor) knew this was his last game as caretaker boss because Stale Solbakken had already been announced as the new man coming in. But, for me, playing in the Premier League was another landmark, even if in truth I wished my first game in it had come sooner. I had left it late, the second half of the final game of the season in what was a three-year spell in the top division.

Waiting to go on, I didn't feel as nervous as in the previous landmarks in my career. I was more experienced now and more ready. I had a quite a bit to do in the game as well and, although maybe I needed to settle for the first few minutes, it wasn't long before I realised that the standard wasn't massively different to what I'd been used to. So I had now played in the Premier League, which nobody can ever take away from me and it was more vital experience in my career.

When I look back now, how do I see all those loan spells? Character-building is what I would say. In total, it was eight different clubs, with so many different managers and team-mates and different approaches and styles. I was spending time heading off to different parts of the country, out on my own, and not really knowing anyone when I turned up. Have gloves, will travel! Sometimes, fans have a very good affiliation with their goalkeeper and then some loan guy arrives and you don't necessarily get those same warm wishes from the start. Things didn't always go well but it toughened me up and gave me the determination to work even harder.

Those first spells at Accrington and Stockport taught me never to take anything for granted when I was back at Wolves with all the nice facilities and people looking after me. It reminded me that I needed to be professional and work even harder to succeed. The other loans also gave me more of a knowledge about football, about being out there on the pitch and making mistakes and learning from them while dealing with the crowds and everything else.

It made me grow up as a player and as a person and taught me how to behave in a football environment and around a changing room while I was involved in the team. I learned how to put my opinion across as well. I always had one but maybe at Wolves and in those first few loans I would hold back before putting it out there. By the time I got to Doncaster, when I wasn't enjoying it, and I didn't think things were being done properly, I was far better placed to say my piece. I developed a voice, a voice in a man's changing room, and took how I had behaved in youth football into that more unforgiving senior environment. If I didn't feel things were right, I was now prepared to stand up and say it was not right, or go away and sit down with someone to talk through why I didn't feel it was right. The loans helped me with that and gave me experience at so many different levels on and off the pitch.

I grew up away from football as well and, through it all, I was always able to see the bigger picture. There was no point me sitting around at Wolves if I wasn't involved and I always wanted to go out and play, even if I wasn't necessarily jumping for joy at the places I was going to.

I had nowhere to call home a lot of the time and although my Dad and Saba came to visit and watch games, I was in hotel rooms for pretty much most of it. I didn't enjoy being away from my family but it made me more battle-hardened. And that bigger picture was feeling that my time at Wolves would always come, even if I didn't really quite know when.

I always wanted to play at Wolves. Maybe once or twice, I thought it might never happen but, for the most part, I kept that confidence that I could go on and become the number one at Molineux. After that loan spell at Doncaster, I was coming up to 26, had a new contract and felt I had been out enough – this had to be my time. I needed to be settled and not moving around anymore. Was I going to be rewarded for all those loan moves? Would the chance come in time before I lost my patience? Well, yes, it would but not with the sort of results any of us could ever have imagined or hoped for.

13

Lost vision

I had also never imagined that I would wake up one day and not be able to see. But that is what I was faced with that morning in Heartlands Hospital, just as I thought I was coming out of the worst of whatever it was that was wrong with me. I could make out shapes but couldn't focus and couldn't see who a person was until they were literally a metre in front of my face. It was one of the scariest parts of the whole experience.

I remember Saba coming to see me that morning and I just broke down again. I'm not sure she could grasp what was going on either. Imagine for a minute waking up without your eyesight and not knowing whether it would ever come back. Not knowing because still, after so many tests, you don't really know what is wrong with you. We were still waiting for the test results but at least I had been starting to feel a little better and the antibiotics had kicked in. Then I was hit with this. I was taken for another scan, pushed down the hospital corridor in my wheelchair while unable to make out any faces or profiles on people that were passing. They were just shapes.

My consultant Manos and the doctor made sure they got me in for an appointment at the Eye Centre as quickly as they could. It felt like chaos to me, worried as I was about what was going on, not feeling well and desperately not wanting to catch any other infections. I was wearing a mask when I left the room and when exposed to any others. I was becoming really anxious now and had enough on my plate without picking up anything else. I had some eye tests but couldn't really see anything or make out the letters on the wall which I was being asked to identify. I was trying really hard to show they were working properly but sadly they weren't and I had to accept it.

One of the doctors giving me the tests then had a really good look in the back of my eyes and told me I had a bleed in both of them. One was worse than the other but even the 'good' one wasn't in great shape. He told me my vision should improve but there were no guarantees about the long-term effects of any damage that had been caused. She couldn't tell me if my sight would ever go back to how it was before. That was very scary. Did I think I might never been able to see properly again? Absolutely. I had no idea it would come back and I certainly hadn't been given any assurances it would. Being able to see, when you have had vision all your life, is something you take completely for granted.

I could recognise Manos and the other consultant, Dr Paneesha, from their shape and profile but, unless anyone else was sitting right next to me, I had no idea who they were. As the days went on and I had now been in hospital for a week, I still needed platelet transfusions to try to get me back to what had become normal. That gave me a really powerful itchy feeling, so I took Piriton to stop that and enable me to sleep better. I was also still suffering with diarrhoea.

Gradually, though, I did start to feel better and a bit stronger and was able to be discharged and carry on resting at home. Before I did, I was told I'd contracted sepsis and, I'll be honest, I had no idea what that was. It didn't sink in how dangerous the condition was and how much risk I had been under. I know there have been lots of TV adverts about sepsis over the last year or so and it was one of those that I saw a couple of months later that made me realise just how severe a condition it is. My doctor said I was lucky I was a relatively fit guy, even with the leukaemia, because, had I not been, I would probably have gone straight into intensive care and it could have been life-threatening.

If there was something vaguely positive, it was the relief of finally knowing what I was dealing with and to know they had it under control, but the eyesight issue was still a concern. When I got home, Mila was coming towards me and I couldn't see her face properly. That was another tough moment after a couple of weeks of seriously tough moments. I started to well up. I honestly thought I might never see the faces of my kids for the rest of my life. Saba had also said that my pupils in my eyes were looking different. If I put the font on really big on my phone and via a certain angle from my left eye, I could just about make out who was calling me. But I wasn't really answering the phone to anyone at that point. Saba was obviously on my favourites list, so it was more straightforward to call her when I needed to. I was more concerned with trying to get better, so I could at least continue with the leukaemia treatment.

The sepsis was a potential side effect from all the treatment because my immune system had been affected. I had also lost another stone since going down with it. It was a stone I didn't really have to lose, having already lost two since being diagnosed. I managed to get myself back up to Manchester and see the doctors who I hadn't seen in the four or five weeks in which the sepsis took hold. They had received all the reports and knew what was going on and had been kept updated by Manos, so I was hoping to be ready to restart the treatment.

In Manchester, I also went to another eye specialist who took a look at the bleeds and confirmed what had been said before; that one eye was 'better' than the other. He also said I wouldn't need surgery and that he expected it to improve but predicting the time-scales was tricky. I was happy to hear that, as even though I understood there were still no guarantees. he gave me confidence that I had a good chance of it coming back to normal.

There wasn't any medication I could take to speed up the recovery and help my vision. Nature just had to take its course. It was still quite bad for a couple of months. Although the left eye was quicker in improving than the right, it was probably still a full four months before I'd say it was back to anything like normal. It did slowly improve but I was struggling to see properly for a good while. And the font is fairly large on my phone even now!

With what had happened, I hadn't really stayed in touch with people for a few months. I had been away from social media and hadn't replied to messages, for the simple reason that I couldn't see them. I knew friends were concerned I had disappeared a little and, eventually, I spoke to Matt Murray and asked him to pass on what was happening. I still didn't want to be the centre of attention and didn't want everyone knowing the full details and how serious it might have been. So I asked Matt just to spread the word that I was fine and getting on with the treatment. He could relay messages without revealing everything and could just let them know there wasn't anything to worry about. In other words, passing on the message that I wasn't okay, but I was okay, and that I was just going through a tough time I needed to come out of.

Back in my room at Christie's, it was still a struggle to see and I asked for a smaller room so I could be closer to the TV. The only way I could keep track of anything else was to put my face to one side and have a lap-top next to me, so I could just about see through my left eye. I imagine I was quite a strange sight to anyone who didn't know what was going on. As I was getting closer to my next phase of treatment and starting to feel stronger, friends came up to see me now and again and if my bloods were okay and we could find somewhere quiet, we'd go out for a bite to eat. I wouldn't be able to read the menu, though, so they'd have to do it for me, which was probably another comedy moment for anyone else who saw it, like the waiters. They must also have noticed that I was trying to focus really hard when speaking to them, so gradually I got used to it and learned to live with it for a while.

Cooking for myself was also interesting. With me being tall, chopping onions and so on, when I couldn't see properly, became a bit of a challenge as to know how close the knife was to my finger. The way things were going, I wouldn't have ruled out chopping my finger off just to add to the fun. My eyesight improved but I wouldn't say there was one particular moment or incident where I noticed it change. There was often a kind of blocked splodge in my vision, so I had to move to see things properly. Over time, that started to reduce and it was difficult to know how much it had improved as I couldn't really remember what it had been like before. My vision must have been good, for me to be a keeper but I was never quite sure when it had returned to normal.

Overall, this was a really tough time, one of the toughest I had, and it was also really frustrating given that I had tried to be so careful about avoiding infections, for obvious reasons. I remember asking Manos how I could have contracted sepsis when I had been so meticulous about everything. He said I had probably caught it via my mouth and that even with taking as many precautions as humanly possible, sometimes you just can't stop it happening. Even so, my reliance on hygiene and caution went to another level after this. It also changed my attitude towards going into the hospital. Previously, if I wasn't in for treatment, even if I was feeling unwell, I would stay in the apartment and fight it because I didn't want to spend any more time in hospital than necessary. That meant the hospital also knew that if I did ring, they would very quickly help me, because they realised my situation must have been pretty bad for me to call.

After the sepsis, I decided I was going to call them straightaway if I didn't feel right and I wasn't going to wait a day or so and hope something would pass. After all, if I hadn't been admitted straightaway when I started feeling poorly with the sepsis, who knows just what might have happened?

14

The tactics board

There were plenty of 'What if's' back at Wolves after our relegation from the Premier League and much wondering about what was going to happen next because the future looked unpredictable. After all the success the club had enjoyed under Mick McCarthy, it all seemed a bit of a mess when he went before Terry Connor was given the job on a caretaker basis. I loved TC, as did all the players, and everyone was willing him to do well. No-one could have done any more in trying to help the club stay up. He also gave me that one and only taste of the Premier League when I went on at Wigan.

It had already been announced that Stale Solbakken was coming in as manager. Nobody really knew much about him and, by that, I mean the players as well as the fans. We were aware he had played in England for Wimbledon and had a very good reputation for his work in Denmark with Copenhagen. Reflecting now, it felt to me like I arrived at Wolves a little bit when he was in charge. It was the first time I felt complete respect from a manager in terms of being given the number one shirt and knowing I was the first choice. I got on well with all the previous managers and had been involved heavily with Mick and TC but this was the time I moved from what people would call a 'young keeper' to more of a man.

I was still only 26 – in many people's eyes that is young for a goalkeeper – but had the chance to make the position my own with Wayne Hennessey still recovering from a long-term injury. It all started with the Carling Cup against Aldershot and another penalty shoot-out, in front of the recently completed new at Stan Cullis Stand. Unlike Chesterfield in my previous Carling Cup appearance, I actually managed to save one this time which helped us to make it through. It was a scrappy win but I went on to start the season really well under Stale, even though there was still a lot of confusion around the club with players wanting to leave and a lot of new faces coming in. By the second international break, we were third in the table and went into that October breather with four clean sheets out of five games to suggest we were solid defensively and had become hard to beat. Sadly, the optimism wasn't destined to last.

Life was very different under Stale and training in particular was a departure from what we were used to. He didn't let the keepers train with the team much but that didn't really bother me. I enjoyed training with coach Pat Mountain and the other goalkeepers – I always had done – so to spend an hour on dedicated keeper training rather than with the team was something I found beneficial. I know that working on shape and formation as a team is always important but, as a goalkeeper, that could sometimes be boring, so I was happy working hard with Pat on different drills and making sure I kept myself in peak condition.

I felt I had a good season in 2012/13, even though it was a disastrous one for Wolves as a team. I know the club's form dipped massively around Christmas and afterwards but I felt good personally, particularly for my first sustained season as the Wolves number one. It didn't work out for Stale after that promising start but I never had a problem with him and I know he has asked after me a few times since my illness which was nice. On the pitch, his methods were probably more suited to European football, where he has had success, and maybe even the Premier League, but not necessarily the Championship. I am not sure he gave that division the respect it deserves for being so competitive and probably unlike any other league you can think of.

I still remember the first League game, at Leeds. The idea for the formation looked good in practice, with us keeping a high line, but teams will just smash it down the channel in the Championship and get in behind you. At Elland Road, with a big and passionate crowd, it was always going to be difficult. They scored an early goal and it just set things off. We had some good results in those early stages but then I think teams worked us out and I don't think our intensity was up to what is needed in such a demanding league. Ultimately, it didn't work with Stale, although would we have stayed up if he had been in charge all season rather than being sacked in January? Yes, possibly. I think we would have won enough games. We maybe just didn't have the grit and spirit to fight for results when we weren't playing well; the ability to grind out three points or snatch a draw from tough games is so important. With the quality we had, it was like we could go out and play teams off the park and, if that didn't work, we would lose.

There were some very talented players coming in to Wolves at that time. Bakary Sako was excellent and someone who would go on to become a real hero at the club. Bjorn Sigurdarson could have been just as exciting and, while it didn't completely work out, if you ever saw him train, you would see why he was brought in. He had everything a footballer needed – pace, power, the ability to score – but just never seemed able to get it all going and work on the pitch in the same way he did in training. Razak Boukari was another who looked so dangerous and, for me, could have been as good or better than Sako but suffered some really bad injuries. I thought Slawomir Peszko was lively and Tongo Doumbia was another who seemed to have much potential. When we played a pre-season friendly at Shrewsbury, he had the look of Patrick Vieira in his performance but, again, it didn't kick on from there when we got into the League action.

There were a lot of players coming in from overseas and I know it sounds like a cliché, and perhaps one Wolves then changed under Nuno, but it can be very tough to adapt to the Championship. Once you reach winter, with all the Saturday-Tuesday games and so many demands, you have to be a certain character to thrive. Although we had some very good players and were third in the autumn, we weren't able to deal with everything going into that winter spell of matches. And we should never have been relegated with so much quality in the team.

Even in that second half of the season when Stale had gone, we had Sylvan Ebanks-Blake and Kevin Doyle up front and should have had more than enough to stay up. It just goes to show that if things inside the changing room or at the club as a whole aren't quite right, then it doesn't matter who you are, or how much quality you think you have, you are not safe from relegation. There was a lot of unrest around Christmas as Stale was in his final weeks and then Dean Saunders arrived. I never saw it like that throughout my time at the club.

There were a few whispers around the dressing room about what was going on and how information was being leaked. We would have a team meeting, then an hour later it would be all over the Express & Star, complete with every bit of detail. Someone was passing information on, which showed that things just weren't right on the inside. It was clear that it was probably a lot to do with how things were at the time and, in that respect, maybe we deserved to go down.

I couldn't let that season pass without mention of an incident which I know I am still very much remembered for. Yes, the infamous tactics board! First of all, some background: Having worked with Dean at Doncaster, I wasn't really sure it was the right decision when he came in to Wolves in the January. Things at Doncaster were always a bit disorganised and I thought it might be the same at Wolves, where it might be even more difficult given it was a much bigger club.

It might have worked, and Dean was certainly as enthusiastic as ever but I wasn't massively convinced. He tried a few different things, which isn't necessarily bad when you are on such a poor run. He moved his office from upstairs to a small room along the corridor downstairs and always liked to keep everyone on their toes. We wouldn't know what time training was from one day to the next, so, if we reported at 9am, we might start at 10am one day and 10.30am the next, or then do something completely different. It might not sound much but I didn't like it. I like to know what I am doing. I like routine, I am a bit 'OCD' when it comes to football and preparation and I'm not the only player who is like that.

If I know we are out training at 10.15, I am in the gym at 9.45, doing the work I need to do to make sure I am in the best condition to train well and reduce the risk of injury. I remember on a few occasions warming up and being ready to go out, then all of a sudden hearing we had a team meeting. Having spent a good half -hour warming up, that meant I would have to sit through a half-hour meeting and get cold and stiff, then go straight out afterwards. That annoyed me but was nothing to do with Dean as a person. And, as you do in football, I just got my head down, stayed focused and concentrated on giving my best.

We had only won once under him by the time we got to the infamous game with Bristol City in the March and that is when the incident happened. There was more build-up around that particular game as well. We had been talking about playing out from the back, and working on it, and Dean would always say that if anything went wrong, it was on his shoulders. He would take the blame. That was giving us licence to take a few risks, although, in truth, and especially with limited practice, we weren't good enough to play out from the back at that time.

We trained at Molineux the day before the game after a last-minute decision to move from the training ground. Friday is an important day for me and I always want to make sure I train properly and get myself completely right for the next day. That 'OCD' coming out again! I had just started to get warm and was only a very small way into my training, when Dean shouted: "Come on everyone, back on the bus. We're going." Some of the other lads might not have been training for various reasons but I hadn't finished what I wanted to do and I certainly didn't want to go into a game without training properly. I was fuming. Maybe it wasn't such a big thing for some players, but for me, that routine, the last training session before a match, was so crucial.

Anyway, then came the game. I passed the ball out to David Davis, as I had been asked to, and, under pressure, he had to knock it straight back to me. The way the ball reared up, I wasn't sure whether to control it with my foot or my knee. As it turned out, I did neither. It squirmed under my foot to give Bristol City the lead, in what was such a massive game for us. Strangely enough, we had played Leeds at home a few weeks before and Jamie O'Hara had whipped a ball back at me in the air, in the middle of the goal, and on my weaker left foot. I'm not too bad on my left but wouldn't necessarily choose taking one in the air in the middle of the goal unless I really, really needed to!

I remember saying to Pat that it was getting ridiculous and that it was going to cost us soon and I would end up looking like a fool. Lo and behold, against Bristol, I did. It was one of those occasions when you want the ground to just swallow you up but, once it has happened, all you can do is put it behind you and get on with the game. As it was, we managed to come back and win 2-1 thanks to Sylvan and Doyler in the second half. Although, of course, I knew nothing about that, as I was on my way to hospital at the time.

As most people now know, it properly went off at half-time but I would say that while I was angry and frustrated, I definitely didn't start it. Going into the changing room, when something like that has happened, you don't need anyone to point it out. I knew exactly what I had done and I knew it would need to be discussed later but at this time I was focused on putting it behind me and moving on into the second half. Dean, having previously said he would carry the can if something went wrong when we were trying to play out from the back, started giving me a bit about what had happened.

Remember, I was still pissed off and frustrated about how things were going for the club and the way everything seemed to be heading. I took my profession very seriously. It wasn't like I could make a mistake and forget about it but I knew what I had done and how I needed to recover. I took everything very personally with my football, I played for Wolves, I loved playing for Wolves, so everything that was going on with the club was very personal for me. Anyway, Dean kept on going: "What the fuck are you doing?" and so on, and, all of a sudden, I just exploded.

I chucked my water bottle across the room and stood up. "Shut the fuck up," I shouted, and from there it all turned into a bit of a melee. Others got in between us with some pushing and jostling and it always makes it look worse when that happens, doesn't it? I don't think I would ever have hit him – he was the manager, after all – but the red mist had come over, 100 per cent. In that situation, in that changing room and in a team environment, I am respectful but, as soon as that button has gone in me, I am done with talking to anyone. It is best then to just leave me alone to calm down.

Everyone was telling us to cool it but that was the last thing I wanted to hear and I didn't want to reason with anybody by this point. Dean kept shouting and I would respond: "Fuck off, Dean, you prick!" I needed to get myself out of the situation and, as I walked out of the dressing room and into the shower area, the tactics board was an easy target. And a far better option than hitting your manager! So I took aim and, whack, gave it a big wallop, right in the middle. What a punch! The problem was, I didn't realise that the board had a metal pole in the back of it and I had caught it beautifully, full on.

As I walked out, I heard the assistant manager Brian Carey say something like: "You should have done that out on the pitch!" That sparked another flashpoint and I came back for some more. I like Bri as well, I got on really well with him but, in the heat of that moment, things can quickly kick off even among people you really like and get on with. He was another who was swiftly told to "go fuck himself".

Nobody came to blows, though, and I got myself out into the toilet area to sit on my own. I was upset, crying with anger and rage as I locked myself in the toilet trying to compose myself. After a few minutes, I had calmed down a bit and took off my glove. Ah shit! My hand was double its normal size. This wasn't good. Once it was off, there was no way I could get the glove back on and I had to walk to the doc's office to tell him my hand was wrecked.

There was no way I could carry on and, while there were a lot of whispers about what had gone on, I think Dean and the club tried to keep it all quiet after the game. By this time, I was on my way to hospital, thinking that was my Wolves career well and truly over. Surely that was me done. No going back. It felt at the time like I wouldn't be able to go anywhere at Wolves now and would have to move on.

On top of that, I nearly had a scrap with my dad. They had called him to tell him what had happened and ask him to take me to hospital, and the steward had added his version. Let's face it, everyone in the tunnel that day would have heard it. He started asking me what the fuck I had done and I didn't want to hear that either, so we had a verbal set-to in the car. The wheels were well and truly coming off – the whole situation had got completely mad and out of control.

I remember while I was waiting at the hospital, I caught up with the final result and received a text from Sylvan. 'All for you, brother', he wrote. That put a smile on my face. Nice one, Sylv! I needed surgery to have the hand pinned and a wire was put in the next day. Seriously tough opponent, that tactics board! I wouldn't recommend going a few rounds with it.

After that, it was all about what would happen to me at Wolves. My season was over and was my career at Molineux going the same way? I hadn't had any contact with Dean and recall going to his office to try to sort things out. I thought he would fine me and wasn't going to have that at all. Although calm, I was still ready for a fight. Verbally, anyway! I was prepared to state my case and have another argument if necessary. To be fair, it never came close to that.

We had a decent chat and Dean explained that, as manager, he couldn't back down in the dressing room despite the fact he said he was shitting himself! I apologised for being so angry, even if I would still stand up for the overall point I was making. Everything that had been going on around the club, losing every week, the build-up of all the tensions…I had taken it personally and that incident was the spark which meant I just couldn't hold back. I couldn't separate my football life from my personal life – they were the same, so I found it hard to leave the football side out of my daily life.

Was the situation resolved? Yes I'd say so. We all make mistakes but, when something happens, if I can go in and be honest with someone and they are also honest with me, then it is all even and we can move on. If Dean had been funny with me about it, or vice versa, a bad situation would have dragged on and things could have turned out very differently. Maybe our relationship was different from then on but we had told each other what we thought and we continued to speak face-to-face. We were fine and while I wouldn't say it was a blossoming working relationship, there was respect on both sides.

Having said that, I still didn't think it was going to help my Wolves future and that, come the end of the season, I might well be on my way. Although I was talking to Dean, it would probably have been very tricky for him to make me his first-choice goalkeeper moving forward. I had some time off while the hand was healing and probably needed it.

As for Dave Davis, did we ever talk about what had happened? A few times, yes. He's a good mate and we have been able to laugh about it since. We referred to him being like a spinner sending down an off-break at Edgbaston which completely deceived me. The way he got some turn on that pass...some talent that. You're in the wrong game, Dave! You have to move on and I remember standing with Pat and the tactics board when the club did a fun video at Christmas a year or two after. As for Dean, he lost his job at the end of the season and, even though I knew him staying could have been the end for me, I still felt for him, as I don't like people losing their job.

The big turning point in that run-in, which I was looking at from the outside, was Sylvan's injury. The win against Bristol City was followed by victories against Middlesbrough and Birmingham, with us scoring three in both, but the Blues game saw Sylvan come off after a tackle from Paul Robinson. It was a bad injury and, as soon as we lost him, I think our hopes of survival had gone. He had been banging the goals in, giving us a lifeline and giving everybody hope that we could stay up. Once we lost him, things spiralled downwards again.

The fans weren't happy, understandably so, but were great with me despite what had happened. I think they felt my frustration. They were obviously not happy about the incident or me being unavailable but, perhaps in strange circumstances, they were able to see there were actually people in the changing room who cared about the situation just as much as they did. Had Sylvan scored the goals to keep us up and Dean had stayed, I certainly don't think I would have remained at Wolves and gone on to enjoy what I did the years after. How football works, eh? Funny old game, as someone once said.

As it was, the club was in dire straits after a double relegation and I wanted to play my part in helping us turn it around.

15

Acceptance

If that situation at Wolves had been taken out of my hands and I had had to leave the club because of what happened, I would have had no choice. But once I knew I could stay, even with the dreadful situation the club had found itself in, there was no way I wanted to leave. And that is me really, I am not the sort to give up on anything.

That is also what kept me going through the leukaemia treatment, in particular after that dangerous episode with the sepsis. Keep riding it, son. Keep riding it! For those few weeks, when I was really struggling, there was still no quit in me. Never would be. As bad as I felt during those weeks – and I felt seriously bad – I just kept believing that it would pass. If I had to sit there and suffer, I didn't mind if I was getting towards the end goal and that was what kept me going through the difficult days of pain.

When you are diagnosed with cancer, a lot of people tell you to keep fighting, which I absolutely understand as a way for them to show you their support. But I'm not sure that is always the right terminology and not in my case. Yes, it is about fighting in a way, but the biggest thing for me was acceptance. That is the main emotion which helped get me through everything. I had to accept that I had cancer. I had to say to the cancer: "I accept you, you are not my enemy, you are just here. I am not planning for you to stay but while you are here, then you are here and I will accept that you are here." That was my thought process because focusing any anger or bad energy on the cancer was of no use whatsoever to me.

To think 'why me', which I admit did cross my mind for a very short time right at the start, would serve no purpose in trying to get to the end goal – recovery. It was more a case, as the title of this book says, of 'Why Not Me'? Why shouldn't I be the same as so many people in life in being diagnosed with a serious illness? So I accepted the situation I was in, I accepted the cancer, because I think when you accept something – whether it's good or bad – you can figure out a way to work with it. Cancer is obviously a horrible thing but I accepted it into my life and I accepted it was part of my path.

It was all about continuing to trust the process, trust what I was doing, trust what I was eating and all the little things I could do, alongside trusting the medical people and the treatment I was receiving. I would also meditate, which was something I had done when I was healthy, just to keep my mind clear. And further down the line, when I had more energy, I would do a five or ten-minute yoga session.

I set out a plan in my head as to the best way to approach what was happening and the best way to try and get better. I'm not saying I could control everything, clearly I couldn't, but I was trying to control the controllables. When you do that, however bad things get, at least you feel you still have that element of control and your actions being important. That was the biggest thing for me. Acceptance. Accepting my emotions. And getting on with doing everything I could to help myself. At times, that wasn't easy, though.

If I was upset or thinking a lot on those long and lonely nights, I might deviate from that mindset and I needed to stop that and get those thoughts out of my head. I might have had some bad thoughts but I made sure I accepted everything and didn't become negative about the overall process. When I could sit back and listen to my own thoughts, I still felt I was in control. If the negativity did come in, it might come in for an hour or so, maybe longer. But I kept thinking there would be a time when I have listened to what those thoughts are telling me but now they have to go away, because my path is different. I wasn't going to let those thoughts take over my mindset and push me in a different direction. That is that outlook which helped me through the entire treatment process.

It was a strange time for me after the sepsis and in the build-up to Christmas. There were times when I felt like crying and breaking down but I had no more tears in me. I think I shed them all in the first couple of days after the diagnosis. There were times when I was a little sad but I've never been a massive crier in any case. That is not say I'm really tough and don't feel any emotion but people show that in different ways, don't they?

I also had to accept that every time I heard the word 'cancer' on television, it made me shudder. I accepted that it was a word that scared me. And when I accepted that it scared me, it actually took the fear away of hearing that word.

Even now, I'd say it probably makes me a bit queasy and it isn't easy to accept emotions like that into your life. But I try and find ways.

I have always been someone who is very grateful for everything I have had in life. During the treatment, I had bad times like anyone does, but would just accept that I was having a bad half hour, a bad half day, or a bad day. I would think 'that's fine', because I knew I still had so many positives to look forward to in life when I was better. When I had those bad times, I would think: 'Do you know what? I am just feeling a bit emotional today, and that is fine'. As long as I was aware of those emotions, I could accept them, and I could deal with them.

I was going down a spiritual path even before the leukaemia and that helped me in how I dealt with it all. I had reached a place where I was feeling very much aligned with my emotions and my thoughts. Before driving in to Wolves for training, I used to wake up early and meditate, maybe between 6.30 and 7am. I was into that process for two or three years before I was diagnosed, although I wouldn't say I was a fully-fledged 'Buddha' or anything like that.

I just discovered at that time in life that it isn't necessarily easy to be happy. It might sound strange, but I think you really have to work on being happy. I felt that if I woke up a few minutes earlier every day and meditated, I could listen to the thoughts in my head. And then, whether I was driving home from training or from anywhere, it felt like I was more in control of my emotions. It helped in my relationship with Saba as well. Like any couple, we had the odd argument and still do. But I think the changed state of mind really helped us both and we now find it far easier to sit back and have a discussion rather than argue.

The other thing that I think happens a lot in modern life is that people develop a fear of things that might actually never happen. They get worked up about something and what it might mean even before it has taken place. So what we become scared about might never occur. That knowledge helped me through the treatment as well; in other words, not getting carried away or worried about what might happen further down the line. Sometimes, you can create a scenario in your head that never happened. I am sure we have all played out a situation or argument with someone that has not even taken place. If you keep thinking and going over it in your head, it develops almost an inevitability that it will happen, certainly in a negative sense. Ignoring all that, and being happy, is actually a process.

When you see someone looking miserable, you might say: "Oh come on, cheer up. Be happy". But it isn't necessarily that simple or straightforward. I truly believe you need to find out what it is that makes you happy and then do it as much as you can. It might only be small things but if you practise them and make sure you do them often, the more likely you are to be happy. That is how I feel.

Sometimes, we can all become lost and feel there is no time or we are too busy with work or something else. When that happens, it helps to just get back to basics and, from there, I set off on my spiritual journey. What was it that made me happy? Maybe it was reading in the morning, or meditating, or listening to a spiritual leader via an audio book on the way into training. I know I have sometimes driven back from training and not remembered my journey as I have just been absorbed in my mind the whole way. At other times, maybe it was going to the gym, or, most important of all, spending time with friends and family, or picking Mila up from school. Things like that are so valuable in bringing with them a sense of perspective. Then, if something bad happens during the day, you can see it for what it is and know, just like my treatment, that it will pass. So when I was struggling, it was a case of: I feel sick today, I'm not dying, that is what it is, and it will move on because tomorrow is another day. Ride it out, son. Ride it out.

Tomorrow is a new day and I have plans for my future that will not be affected by this cancer. I just need to accept it and get through this period, get to where I want to be and where I know I will be happy. Even when I was at my lowest ebb – and there were a fair few times like that during the treatment process – I would accept the cancer. Because I knew that the end goal was a life still to spend with Saba and my kids and the chance to follow my dreams.

16

Steadying the ship

It wasn't exactly the stuff of dreams at Wolves after the double relegation from the Premier League all the way to League One. More like a nightmare, in the football sense anyway. With Dean Saunders having left, which I thought gave me a chance to stay, Kenny Jackett came in as the new head coach. And, while it might be strange to say after such a difficult couple of years, very quickly the club seemed to be brought back together.

The place had been on its knees. Failure on the pitch, dressing room unrest and no any guarantees that League One would be a walk in the park. Many other big teams had found it difficult down there and sometimes it can be tough to stop downward momentum. But that League One season turned out to be the start of an exciting revival which I think has gone on to the current day.

Kenny knew what he was about and knew what he wanted. Straightaway, he told us we needed to get that link back between us and the fans. There had been such a massive disconnect, with stories leaked and the fans unhappy with the players. We all know what a difference the Wolves supporters can make, and in such numbers, but they hadn't had much to cheer about over that previous couple of years. Kenny said how that relationship seemed to have completely disappeared and he wasn't wrong.

I remember he tried to meet as many fans as he could that summer and we also went on a run through the city centre as part of pre-season training. It was all small steps towards trying to win back the confidence of the supporters. When I look back, I think the deterioration in the relationship had begun during the last Premier League season. Then Mick McCarthy had been sacked and, from there, everything just got worse.

It was now all about trying to get that link back, make it strong and then hopefully move the club forward again. I knew it wouldn't be easy because other big clubs had not been able to lift themselves out of that division very quickly. We were going to be a big scalp, with others raising their games and desperate to put one over on us.

As Kenny came in, it looked like it would be me and Wayne Hennessey fighting for the shirt. I was thinking it was going to be another tough battle – I knew how good Wayne was – but I also looked on it as starting afresh under a new manager, especially after how my previous season had ended with a broken hand. Wayne was coming back from problems, too, and needed a run of games to get back to his best having suffered two cruciate knee injuries. It wasn't long before he went to Yeovil for a three-month loan to build up his match sharpness.

That gave me an opportunity to start the season and, if I did well, to keep my place, which is how it turned out. I can still remember our first game, away to Preston. I'm not sure whose idea it was but we started this habit towards the end of the warm-up of applauding the fans before we went back to the dressing room. There were about 5,000 Wolves fans there that day and, remember, this was our first competitive game since the dreadful ending at Brighton as we were relegated from the Championship.

I wasn't at Brighton but know from talking to the lads what an awful afternoon it had been. Now, a few months later, none of us completely knew how the fans were going to react. But, when we applauded them at the end of that warm-up, the roar that came back was something else. It was an incredible noise, which I think was their way of telling us that they were right back behind us and ready to give us the support we needed. It was almost like, they knew we had been struggling and had hit rock bottom but now they wanted to back us again. In other words: "We've been through all this crap together, now it's time to get things going." It was music to our ears.

Later in the season, almost 9,000 travelled to see us at MK Dons, which is incredible. I think they were just ready to back the club again because they could see what everyone was trying to do and to move on from some of the mistakes and difficult situations of the previous year or so. It was a tough old game at Preston but we managed to come away with a hard-fought goalless draw and were off and running with a point.

Once everything settled down, which it did quickly, I knew we had the potential to have way too much quality for League One. I know there was a lot of talk about the 'bomb squad' and the players that needed to leave, as well as a question mark over the future of Bakary Sako. But we quickly found a rhythm, had a great team and a lot of the young lads had their chance to shine. Kenny wanted to put a lot of emphasis on youth – in fact, that was the message throughout the club, with plans in place to build the new Academy - and the fans went for it.

It wasn't just about the young players though. Macca (Kevin McDonald) came in and was running things in midfield, Sam Ricketts as skipper, Danny and Stears (Richard Stearman) looked good together in defence, Dave Edwards provided goals and experience. So many of those more experienced lads led by example. Eddo is one of the best professionals I have ever worked with. He was just constant, working as a top pro every single day. Danny was the same, Sam, myself, doing extras in the gym.

Yes there were discussions and team meetings but I think it is always important to practice what you preach as well and the younger lads could see what we were doing and how we would conduct ourselves around the training ground and on a matchday.

If you're a young player, wanting to learn, and you see the likes of Sam and Eddo doing extra work after training, then you quickly realise that is the rightthing to do.

Leigh Griffiths was scoring goals in the early part of the season as well and although every game was tough and we were very much up there to be shot at, I always felt we had a great chance of achieving something that season. Imagine if I had left before all this happened. If Dean had stayed, it would probably have meant I would struggle to feature. Instead, I had the best years of my career from that point and could have missed it all, certainly from a Wolves point of view. That's football. It can be so strange sometimes. Timing is everything! It is all about taking the opportunities when they come along and making the most of circumstances. Control the controllables!

By now, I was 27 and the likes of myself, Eddo, Sam, Danny were taking more responsibility around the place. I was more of a senior player and it was down to us to help the young lads through, like Griff, Pricey (Jack Price), Evo (Lee Evans), Dave Davis, Doc (Matt Doherty) and Ethan Ebanks-Landell. I really enjoyed that step-up and change to my role in the dressing room. I felt ready for it. I was far more comfortable making decisions and speaking up.

From that time and right up to when I finished in football, I was involved or asked for my opinion if there was any meeting going on or anything to do with the players and the changing room. It was a case of watching over the dressing room and looking at what other people were doing a little bit more. Not in any bad or negative way, just trying to help the younger lads out if I could. Maybe just suggesting things like when and what to do in the gym, making sure people warmed up properly, doing things right outside of football. I was becoming more of a mentor and that was a role I relished.

It happens that way in football as you become more experienced and it was only the same as the way all those experienced lads at Wolves had looked out for me when I was younger. It was a very different story as a young player, which for me meant going into a Premier League dressing room when I was sitting on the bench as a 17-year-old. I might have been confident later on but I wasn't so confident going in at that age.

At that point, I just got on with everything quietly and made sure I minded my own business. Sit there in the corner, read the match programme and don't speak unless you are spoken to! Michael Oakes, as the senior keeper, was really good with me and the goalkeeping coach Bobby Mimms was good, too. A couple of others like George Ndah and Shaun Newton would look after me as well, and Matt Murray. All the senior pros were okay to be fair but some would pay you more attention than others. It is a very different dynamic being a young player than someone a bit older.

All of it was being led at the top by Kenny Jackett, who was just what the club needed at that time. I would say he – and I mean this in the nicest, possible way – almost has a bit of 'OCD' about him. I need to say that I really like him, I loved working for him and have the utmost respect for him. But when you worked for him, you soon came to realise that everything had its place and needed to be done properly. You knew with Kenny that his mind was always thinking about the next game, or the next training session, and he absolutely lived and breathed football.

When I was in the gym, sometimes I'd see his head peeping through the window – he was always looking around the place and making sure he was aware of what we were doing. He'd keep an eye on what we were having for lunch and what we were doing after training. I actually think he wanted us to live like monks! I'm fairly sure he mentioned that in his opening talk to the squad.

He said we were not supposed to be drinking any alcohol until the following June. That got a bit of a giggle in the changing room, I can tell you! I think he maybe came in and thought there was a drinking culture at the club with a few things that had gone on before and the story about Roger Johnson which made the press. There definitely wasn't a drinking culture and, even if I don't think many players – if any – went through the season without a drink, we understood the need for high standards.

We knew that if there was an opportunity to let off a bit of a steam and go out and enjoy ourselves, it needed to be done at the right time and in the right way. When he made that speech, it was just before the pre-season tour when you are normally given a night out as a reward for the hard work. It felt like we had been running solidly for four weeks or so and we were wondering when we might get a release. No such luck, unfortunately!

Kenny was under a lot of pressure to get us up that season and everything he did was meticulously structured. He was big on professionalism and was very good in that regard and was just what the club required at that time. He had the players' respect, even if it sometimes felt like he constantly had his foot on my neck! We could be absolutely flying in the league and working really hard in training but we wouldn't get a day off if it didn't fit in with the overall plan.

I recall some of the senior lads, myself included, having to go and play Manchester United under-19s after we had been promoted. That went down like a lead balloon. Why did he do that? I'm not sure. Although I think he was obsessed with the lads not having too much time on their hands before the end of the season and taking our foot off the gas. It probably worked, too, as we went on to finish the season strongly and set plenty of club and League records.

Kenny's approach was excellent and he got us playing football again in some difficult conditions which you can get in League One. We had grit as well, so no-one was going to bully us. Everyone knew we could play and we had enough to be able to battle our way through to wins as well as playing teams off the pitch.

Macca coming in was such an influence. He was so comfortable on the ball, he would demand it even in tight situations and his contribution meant we could change our style. I think later in Kenny's time we had to shut up shop a bit, more due to budget constraints, but we really attacked that League One season and, even with all the rough and tumble, played some great football.

Like with Mick McCarthy and Terry Connor, Kenny had a good partnership with his assistant, Joe Gallen. I'd say Kenny was a bit strange, in the nicest possible sense, and although we would have disagreements, I still really like him now. It was very formal and if you wanted to speak to him, it would be in his office and pretty much only ever about football. Joe was the man in between, who would talk to all the players about all sorts of things. You could sound him out about what Kenny might be thinking and I am sure Joe was doing the same, getting information to feed back to Kenny.

I remember in the early days I'd come in on a Monday and Joe would be like: "What did you get up to over the weekend?" My response would be simple. "Nothing!" In the back of my mind I'd be thinking: 'Can I really trust you yet?' Maybe towards the end of that season, it had progressed to: "We just had a few, Joe, nothing crazy!"

Those are the sort of football relationships which build over time and you work out who you can trust. As well as being a very good coach, Joe was a character who all the players got on really well with.

He and Kenny had a nice balance, which is why their partnership worked so well and continued to do so in their first couple of seasons at Portsmouth. It was great to work with them at Wolves and, coming in after such a turbulent time with the double relegations, it felt like an air of normality had returned.

17

"Go well, mate..."

Normality also returned for me after the really tough time I had with sepsis and, having got back to some sort of reasonable condition, I was able to continue with my treatment. We were coming to a point when I was told there would be a six-week cycle which could be the most testing part of the chemotherapy. And I felt I'd had a fair bit to deal with already!

It was all about when I was ready to take it on and there was always that little spell of waiting. At this time, in the build-up to Christmas, my bloods just weren't coming up again at all. When that happened, especially when it went on for a while, there was a worry as to why they weren't responding. Was there something wrong? Was the treatment not working? What was going to happen next? Aside from that, I was feeling okay; nothing like well but as good as I could be in that situation.

You can receive medication to boost your white cells, stimulants and injections to give them a kick, but it doesn't always make an immediate difference. And there is nothing that can be done to boost your platelets – they will just come up when they are ready. They have to reach a figure of 75 and your neutrophils have to be at 0.7 before you can start treatment again. It was a case of waiting – and hoping that the counts had improved. Several times, they hadn't. So I had a six or seven-week break between treatments and at one point came home to Birmingham for a few days.

It was then that I received a completely random act of kindness that made a really big difference. It felt cold in my house and I was feeling the cold a lot during the illness. The fireplace in our main room wasn't working properly and needed looking at. Normally, when something like that happens, I would never ring someone or look online for a local tradesperson to fix it. It was usually via word of mouth, or someone I knew, that we were able to get repairs done. But the way I was feeling, I didn't want to see anyone I knew.

I wanted it done straightaway and needed someone to do the whole job, not half of it and then come back a few days later. I looked online and rang a local guy who came to have a look. He checked it out and said he wouldn't be able to do it straightaway as he needed a couple of parts but said he would come back next day to do the job. I had never met him before and didn't mention anything about being a footballer, or having leukaemia. It turns out he was called James and he came back again as promised, with his son.

Maybe I was naïve to think he wouldn't recognise me and that, if he did, that he wouldn't know the situation I was in. He did know, or he had found out, and brought me a gift of a boomerang with a letter attached to it. James had been travelling in Australia and hand-crafted the boomerang, and had written the letter since we first met. He was willing to give me this boomerang which had a lot of sentimental value. It was proper touching to think someone could give me something like that, with so much thought behind it.

He had gone home, thought about my predicament and done something which was meaningful, for me and him. The letter read: 'Apologies for not getting the job done yesterday. I needed parts and in any case it is a two-man job. I have brought my son to give me a hand with things while I get you back on. His dream is to be a footballer. He is 21 and I advised him to pack in his job and focus on his dream. I am his Dad after all. He can spend the rest of his life doing something else if he doesn't make it. If you have any advice to give to him, it would be greatly appreciated. I hope you don't mind but I would like to give you a token of my humanity. I spent some time in the Australian outback with the Aborigines and picked, shaped, filed, painted and stamped the boomerang until it became what you now have in your hand. The reason I wanted to give you it is because I made it Down Under, which is where you might feel you are at times. We both know what a good boomerang does…it comes back when you throw it. I have a feeling this will happen to you. You must be strong-minded to have achieved what you have done in your life and you are currently going through the biggest challenge you have ever had to face. But the mind is the most powerful weapon you have, use it to your advantage. And, like a good boomerang, come right back. Put it somewhere that will remind you of your strength when you see it and, as Rocky Balbao once said: "I didn't hear no bell!" Go well, mate, there ain't no fat lady singing in this house.'

Saba started crying when she read it because it just gave us faith that there were still a lot of really good-hearted people out there. I don't think we hear enough of that in life. Instead, so much is about all the negative crap that goes on in the world. The experience for me of a complete stranger not mentioning anything at first but coming back with a gift and really poignant message was incredible.

I don't think James is a Wolves fan. I'm not even sure if he is a football fan or has a team. But his son was an aspiring footballer and was after some advice. That was another thing which really struck home with me. James told him to go for it, to pack in his job and go for his dream. You don't hear enough about that these days either, do you? Usually, it's the opposite, a safety-first approach. But why not give it everything to see if you can achieve what you have set your heart on? His son was a lovely young man and to have that backing from his Dad, I just remember thinking: 'What a guy'. The whole story about being in the outback, what he did for me, his approach with his son, it really touched me.

It was December, five months into the treatment, and even though I was feeling okay compared with previously, I probably didn't look well and certainly not like I had done before the leukaemia. I still couldn't do much physically. I couldn't help James with anything on the fireplace or even help him carry the parts into the house. My mum was having to move stuff in my apartment and help me and Saba with the shopping as I just wasn't strong enough. That was hard for me and there were times when my mum was doing jobs and carrying things and people were probably wondering why I wasn't helping. I remember she had to say something to someone at one stage. She doesn't hold back!

So while I was generally doing well mentally, there were still times I needed perking up and this was one of them. It came at absolutely the right time as well. I had received such fantastic support from everyone – family, friends, Wolves fans, the world of football – but this gesture from a complete stranger really made a difference. I never expect anything from anyone. I know you have to work damned hard for everything you get and work at friendships and so on. So to get this boost when I did was just perfect. Even now, I read that letter again from time to time and still get a lump in my throat.

I had good days and bad days during treatment but was always pretty solid in trying to make the best of the bad times. I would never say no to something that would give me a boost, though, because even on the days I was functioning well, it was still only 40 or 50 per cent of what I used to be. I might say I was alright but even at those alright times, I couldn't properly leave the house, couldn't help anyone and couldn't even make my own dinner. Maybe I could pop out very quickly or grab some food but going out like it was a normal day and going about my business? That just wasn't possible.

I am always a great believer that everything happens for a reason. I could have had anyone round to look at the fireplace. The first company I might have found might not have been James. It could have been Bob or Dave from any other firm who came in and did a great job and that would all have been fine. Yet there were things that occurred during my treatment which seemed to come along at just the right time and the boomerang was one of them. I don't believe it just happened that I stumbled on James's number or that it was a co-incidence. Sometimes, you just get signs of where you are going.

Although I never thought I wasn't going to make it, getting that boomerang and letter just re-affirmed in my mind that my journey was going the way it should. Whatever way that would prove to be, it was all aligning and moving forward.

There were other examples during my treatment when things happened and people came into my life at just the right time. I would often, especially when I was struggling, get a taxi from my apartment in Manchester to Christie's. It would be an Uber, so I'd never know who was going to pick me up. The drivers would often make conversation and ask if I was travelling to hospital to work. With how weak I was feeling, I'm not sure I looked capable of doing much but it was just a way of getting the conversation started. Most of the time, I'd try and brush the question aside, just because I wasn't really up to having a chat. I also never really knew what to say – telling a stranger you have cancer is hardly a normal start to a day. Might make things a bit awkward, you know.

One day, though, the driver asked me and I decided to tell him I was heading to Christie's for treatment for leukaemia. We chatted and it turned out that his young son, I think he was maybe seven or eight, had been treated for ALL – Acute Lymphoblastic Leukaemia – exactly the same as me. He had gone through the same process, exactly the same struggles, and his dad had done everything he possibly could to help his son get back on his feet. He had been working nights so he could be there for his son and family during the day, knowing he needed to earn to keep everything going. And the good news – the best news – was that his son was now doing really well. He had recovered, was in remission and had even taken part in a running event. That was such a positive conversation, coming as it did early in the treatment process when I was starting to struggle with the side-effects.

I had been going through all the feelings and emotions with the diagnosis and treatment, and this was hearing it from a different perspective. There is always someone worse off and this guy had not only had to deal with the worst possible news but had had to do everything he could to keep his family functioning. Imagine working nights while being really worried about his son and his family, then running round in the day sorting out everything. It reminded me again just what my family must have gone through and the stress they were under. I can't begin to imagine what it would be like to have one of your kids diagnosed.

They had all been through the mill and his son was still having check-ups but this was another positive for me, to know people did come through on the other side. The guy picked me up by chance again a few months later and we shared a full update of how we were getting on. It was all very comforting and motivating to understand that so many people went through situations like this in different contexts. I was physically tired, just trying to get through each day, and that sort of thing was really important, just to give me another push and another reminder of what it was I was fighting for. Another important moment in the journey.

Having good positive conversations with people I knew was always vital and I would really value them. Yet when someone really opened up to me and I didn't know and had never met them before, it was very touching. This guy, just like James and the boomerang, didn't have to be anything to me or do anything for me – they didn't owe me anything. But they took the time to talk and help and that sort of thing makes such a difference when you are going through it. The kindness of strangers really can make such a massive impact and offer a reminder of how many truly good people there are in the world.

There were never any guarantees I was going to get better, despite my mentality but, as long as I felt I was on the right path and these little markers came along from time to time, it strengthened my belief in the process. James and the boomerang came just before I was heading into the biggest spell of treatment and after I had been through a very bad period. I was getting into the thick of it now, so this was a good time for this gesture. It was effectively half-time in the schedule. I still have that boomerang, sitting on my bookshelf, with pride of place.

And, there still ain't no fat lady singing in my house…

18

Wolves roar back

For Wolves, our very own boomerang impression came as we soared back from League One in 2013/14 in a great season in which we put right some of what had gone on before. We won the title in very convincing style. I have mentioned Kenny Jackett and Joe Gallen's style of management and the fact so many young players were brought in. It all worked out really positively from that solid start at Preston and there were so many highlights, plus a fair few flashpoints.

We had some good wins early on and were scoring a lot of goals but weren't having it all our own way. Leyton Orient and Peterborough also made great starts and it was proving to be a high standard at the top of the table. I also remember the game at Colchester in the October. We played really well and were 3-0 up going into the final five minutes, when a penalty was awarded against me for a foul on Marcus Bean. I didn't think it was a foul and thought it was a really harsh decision, not for the first time in my career. I was even booked, so that was a further insult. Freddie Sears took the penalty, I saved it and lost it a bit in going bonkers with the celebration.

I think I forgot where I was for a moment and overlooked the fact we were 3-0 up and were going to win the game even if it had gone in. It was right in front of the Wolves fans, who were also going crazy, and I remember everyone jumping on me and me getting really angry and pushing them off. I was just angry with everyone for those few seconds. Why did I react so much when it didn't mean too much in the context of the game? Like all goalkeepers and defenders, I wanted a clean sheet. You put so much work in during the week, working on everything connected to the game and, for us, it's all about trying to keep the opponents out. It looked like I was about to lose that, so I wasn't happy. And for most of us goalkeepers, saving a penalty is the nearest we ever get to scoring a goal. It was a bit embarrassing when I watched the incident back later. There wasn't any need to go that crazy. But I was in the zone, hyped up, in the moment, whatever you want to call it. I wanted my clean sheet, so that's my excuse and I'm sticking to it.

That was a good win for us and we had a couple more 3-0 wins in successive away games in the February at Brentford and Walsall. These games stick out in that season for very different reasons and also formed part of the nine-game winning streak which set a new club record. We went to Brentford when they were top of the table and, if you talk about our winning run, they had gone 19 League games unbeaten, which was an incredible sequence. It felt like a proper big game, a top-of-the-table clash with a massive atmosphere, and was potentially a pivotal day in the season. It was a test we passed with flying colours, taking the lead through James Henry at the end of a tight first half and then Michael Jacobs adding two fantastic goals in the second. It was a resounding way to end Brentford's run and was a big step for us, but the job was not done yet. Nowhere near, in fact.

The three points lifted us above Brentford but only into second in the table because Orient had won as well and were now top. The Walsall game hit the headlines for entirely different reasons and not just with home fans invading the pitch to confront Nouha Dicko after he scored our opening goal and celebrated in front of their stand. It was a passionate local derby and we hadn't played each other in the League for a long time. We had already beaten them on penalties at the start of the season in the Johnstone's Paint Trophy, when Aaron McCarey played in goal, but then lost in the League at Molineux a couple of weeks later. So there was a big build-up and not a lot of love lost between the two sets of supporters.

It was a spicy game anyway but I had been racially abused at Walsall in a pre-season friendly previously and it happened again during this game. I should point out that nothing much really offends me in life. If people say things that aren't right, I just think they are idiots and move on. I know for a fact that a lot of the stuff that comes at you from the stands comes from people who wouldn't dare say it if they walked past you in the street. Anyway, we won well and, at the end, I gave a little 'shush' gesture to the Walsall fans behind my goal.

I'd been getting verbally abused all game, which is fairly standard for a goalkeeper. You get very used to it. I'd say you find a lot of it funny and that was the case with 99 per cent of what I heard that afternoon. But there was one guy being racist and I remember thinking: 'Don't react, don't say anything. Win the game and have your time after that'.

It was pissing me off but I managed to keep control and maintain my concentration, then I went to pick my towel up from the net at the final whistle and gave it the 'shush' gesture. The Walsall fans weren't particularly happy with that and it all seemed to go off. All of a sudden, the police were on the pitch, Walsall keeper Richard O'Donnell was in my face and Azza (Aaron McCarey), our substitute keeper, had got himself right in the thick of it. It was probably him dancing on the pitch that played a part in the altercation! Richard is a proper nice guy as well. I didn't know him too well then but I do now and don't have any problem with him. Maybe Azza had been doing a few things to wind the crowd up and it is one of those situations you get in football, which was mainly handbags but all connected with the passion of the game. At least the police weren't there to chat about my dodgy travel passes from all those years earlier!

Then there was a phone call a Walsall fan made after the game to BBC Radio WM, where she accused me of sticking my fingers up at the fans behind my goal. That was absolute rubbish and with some of the stuff that was said afterwards, I took the decision to speak out and gave a statement outlining what had happened during the game. Normally I just get on with things and move on but I am always honest and some of the things I was accused of wound me up to the extent I felt I needed to have my say and explain to everyone why I had given the 'shush' gesture. It had certainly not been abusive. That phone call from the Walsall supporter, which I think the Wolves fans still talk about to this day, was played in our dressing room on the Monday morning and caused a fair bit of fun among the boys.

Football is an emotional game, that is why we all love it so much, and that was a particularly emotional local derby. Nothing was done afterwards as the perpetrator couldn't be found and it is important for me to say I have absolutely no problem with Walsall at all. I think they are a great club, with great fans, and have no grudge as this was just one person and the sort who I am sure sadly exists at most clubs in the country. It also happened at Stockport once when I was playing there and I think there is still an issue with racist abuse towards players which needs sorting out. I don't think the authorities do enough within the game to stamp it out and recall once having a bit of an argument with an FA representative about it. She had come in to give us the pre-season talk about discipline, which players get every year, talking about any changes in the rules or anything the powers-that-be were looking to highlight or improve within the game.

It emerged that the standard suspension for spitting was seven games but it was only five for racial abuse. I found that staggering. Spitting is disgusting and no-one ever wants to see it but, for me, racially abusing someone affects a far bigger audience. Racial abuse effectively means abusing and alienating a whole race. We had a lively old discussion in that meeting and I certainly put my points across. A lot of people are working on it as it keeps happening and I really hope they can put a stop to it one day so we don't hear of any players getting racially abused.

I feel like football has got it wrong time and time again. There have been times when they didn't have to show leniency but they have let players, fans and clubs get away with examples of racism. And, as has been pointed out, the way players like Raheem Sterling have been treated in the media has also been a big factor. You can create a monster at times and fuel ancient stereotypes but, when it all boils down to it, we all value the same things, whoever we are. We all want a warm place to sleep, to be safe, and to have the best for our children. That is what we all need to remember.

On the pitch, those results at Brentford and Walsall, and the winning sequence they were part of, pushed us into a great position in the race for automatic promotion and one from which we were able to go on and seal the deal. A 2-0 win at Crewe secured promotion and sparked a massive pitch invasion by our fans and it was great to know all the hard work had been worth it.

We had made an immediate return to the Championship but there was still a fair bit of drama and excitement to come. The next game, at home to Rotherham on Good Friday evening, turned into one we will never forget. It was one of the maddest matches I have ever played in and one of the best as well, as we ended up winning 6-4. There were more pitch invasions as well, it was all a bit crazy, end-to-end in front of another full house and incredible atmosphere. Every time we thought the game was over, it wasn't and Rotherham came back, which was no surprise as they were a good team who were right up there in the race for promotion and would eventually win the play-offs. But we managed to get another three points in the bag.

We were desperate to go on and win the title, just like the Championship squad of 2008/09. Kenny would never let us rest on our laurels and I remember he came up to me after we had earned promotion and asked me what I thought.

"Is it holiday season?" he said. "Time to relax?" My response was along the lines of: "Not at all". We wanted to win the league. Knowing Kenny, I think that was his way of finding out what our plans were for celebrating and making sure we were still very much 'on it'. No-one was ever going to down tools but there is that natural relief when you win promotion and you have to be professional and focused to keep going for the big prize.

We followed that Rotherham game with a great win at Orient, who for a long spell had been our very close rivals for promotion but ended up in the play-offs. This was another big and tough game and I remember clattering into Richard Stearman at one point and needing a bandage to stem the flow from a nose bleed. I clashed with Danny Batth going for another ball – it was a proper, gutsy game. We won 3-1 and sealed it with a late long-range goal from James Henry, which had me running two-thirds of the length of the pitch to join in the celebrations.

Our game was the early kick-off and it was on the bus journey home we found out we had won the title, as Brentford had failed to beat MK Dons. We erupted in celebration and, for the first time that season, it was approved that we could have a drink. Or maybe it was just that Kenny wasn't on board.....I can't completely remember. Anyway, we stopped off to get a few beers and enjoyed the rest of the trip knowing that the job had well and truly been done now and we were going to be crowned League One champions.

There were still two games to go and it was good that we were able to pick up four points with a draw at Coventry and a 3-0 win against Carlisle on the last day when Molineux was rocking again. After that, we returned to Molineux a couple of days later for a civic reception and Jody Craddock's testimonial when a Wolves XI was taking on a Sunderland XI. Bank Holiday weekends are often big for me and I often took Sunday as my day to switch off completely in one way or another. Well, we went out after the Carlisle game to toast our great season and the celebrations carried on into Sunday, when I went into Digbeth in Birmingham – always good value on a Bank Holiday. I'm fairly sure Sylvan would have been with me, although the memory is a bit hazy for some reason. I managed to get myself into Molineux on the Monday with very little sleep and looking completely the worse for wear but played a few minutes of the testimonial. It was a great event, with fans from both teams turning out, and I was keen to turn out for such a top bloke as Jody. But I also remember thinking I couldn't wait to get home afterwards after such a heavy weekend.

I really enjoyed that League One season. The team broke a lot of records, both for Wolves and beyond, and I was delighted to play a part in the League clean sheet record, which we achieved with 25. That was 22 from me and three from Azza. We had been confident about the season but knew it wouldn't be easy and would take a lot of really hard work because we were up there to be shot at. As a result, we were delighted we did such a good job and made it such a memorable campaign.

Both from a team point of view and individually, it was nice to have our names in history, even though it hadn't been in the division that any of us had wanted to be in. At least we managed to set some records and hopefully they will always be remembered, in a positive way and as a positive part of Wolves' history. Hopefully the achievements of that team will be highly thought of, in stopping the decline and paving the way for what has followed since with the incredible progress which the club has made.

19

No quit in me

It was all about trying to stay positive in my treatment as well and that boomerang gift had provided me with the boost I needed heading into one of the most concentrated phases of chemotherapy. It was a time for stepping things up and having chemo pretty much every day for six weeks, which was far more intense than I had experienced previously. It was going to be a very lengthy period of treatment and I remember my mum being worried about it – in fact, everyone was.

For about three months after the sepsis, I saw very few people as I was desperate to avoid picking up any more infections. It was coming up to Christmas but I was just keen for it get going.

I wasn't really bothered about Christmas. I know it was Maya's first one but she wasn't going to remember it and I was just focused on getting better. Just like I had been about starting the process before she was born, I wanted to give everything to the treatment as quickly as possible, so I could be around for far longer than just her birth or first Christmas. I remember coming home to Birmingham on Christmas Eve and then going straight back to Manchester and Christie's on Boxing Day. Don't get me wrong, it was really nice to see the kids and the family over Christmas and great to see Mila having a good time but I wasn't right, so it was never going to be like a normal celebration.

I spent a lot of Christmas Day in bed, washed out, and although I managed to come down for dinner, I was feeling rough. The feeling of nausea is one of the worst side-effects during long cycles of chemotherapy but, on the plus side, it was around now that my vision started to improve and my eyes were starting to function properly again. If only I wasn't feeling completely shattered and needing regular blood transfusions!

I was generally managing to cope with that okay and there was only once I had a bit of an illness which meant a stay in hospital. That was in the January when another side-effect really kicked in – one I had never experienced before. I was having real problems going to the toilet, for a 'number two' if you get my drift, and was starting to get real pain in my backside. That made things really difficult.

There was one time when Saba was up to see me and she had brought the kids but I wasn't feeling great with suffering what I'd call a mini illness within the overall illness. I was in absolute agony – every time I went to the toilet, it felt like razors were coming out. I couldn't walk properly and the pain was unbearable. I would manage to go to the toilet, then find myself having to crawl back to the bed. Saba did everything she could to help but I just wanted to be left alone and didn't want to get a doctor or a nurse in. No fuss, please, I can handle this. Crawl back into bed, bite down on my pillow and just get on with it. Ride it out son, ride it out.

On this one occasion, I was thinking if I could get through for 20 minutes or so, the pain would pass. As things turned out, it didn't. Saba had to go but told the nurse the state I was in when she left and, even if I didn't really want her to, I am glad she did. The pain wasn't going away and I don't think I'd have asked for help, even with what I have said before about thinking I would be more open about any problems after the sepsis. I thought I'd be able to fight it but I couldn't and the nurse came in and gave me some morphine which sent me straight off to sleep. It provided some rare and much-needed respite from the pain but this was the sort of problem that carried on for a few months; side-effects to the brutal treatment I needed to save my life. The problem is that if you have any sort of problem or tear in your body, nothing can heal while you are undergoing such strong treatment as chemotherapy.

It was around this time that I remember trying to take Mila to Argos across the road from the apartment. It would normally be a simple enough task; taking my daughter somewhere to do something normal. It must have been 50 metres maximum from the entrance of the apartment complex and I managed to get her there and back but was in absolute agony. I just collapsed into bed afterwards as another reminder that I was a long way off being able to do normal, everyday activities. Not being able to do such basic things also made me feel I wasn't like a father any more. All I had wanted to do was buy a little treat for my daughter, which all of a sudden felt like such an impossible task. I remember lying on the bed, not only in real pain but also feeling guilty that I just wasn't there for her.

I'd say I was on the morphine for around three months. It wasn't something I wanted to rely on because it made me drowsy but there were times that I had no choice. And I just didn't want to go to the toilet, because I knew what was coming. I would fully undress to go because I would be in so much pain that I would end up really sweating. It was so difficult for my mum to see and hear me struggling so much. There was blood every time I went for about three months or so and there was nothing that the medical people could do to help me. It would only heal if I stopped the treatment but I needed the treatment to help fight the disease which otherwise could kill me. That's a nice Catch 22, eh?

So I'd take the morphine to try and offset the pain and I'd sometimes take some in the morning just to help me get into the apartment lift and out to the taxi. And I'd have to do the same after a day's treatment just to be able to get back to the apartment, and then again before going to sleep. There were times when I would feel a little bit better but I'd say they were only moments and things would change very quickly and I'd be back suffering a lot of discomfort. I'd be having baths at least three times a day as well to try to soothe the pain.

At first, I had probably been guilty of playing it all down. The difficulties had started not long after the sepsis but it was manageable then. Up to Christmas, I'd maybe have a good week and then a bad one but it came to the stage in the New Year when it was difficult all the time. There were occasions when the doctor couldn't even look at it and examine me because I was in so much pain. It was just another of the problems that were thrown at me and there were so many difficult moments during the months of treatment. But, for pain, this was probably as bad as it got. I generally have a high threshold but that was as bad as anything I have experienced. It took ages for the problems with my backside to be resolved. It wasn't until about the October, a few months after I completed the treatment, that it cleared up completely. Over time, it had become better and more manageable but would still cause me one or two problems.

There was also a time when Saba actually caught me when I was passing out. No easy thing to do, that, even though I had lost a fair bit of weight! She was up to see me for the weekend and I had woken up and walked to the toilet. Then, bang, I was gone, completely blacked out. It was very fortunate she was there and jammed me between the wall and her arm. I still don't quite know how she did it but she managed to stop me falling and possibly doing myself serious damage. A similar thing had happened earlier when I had been about to sit on the toilet and the seat broke my fall. It was just another side effect of my blood cells not producing in the way they should. I was going to feel light-headed at times.

Mila had seen me unsteady on my feet and I remember her saying: "What's wrong with my Daddy, what's wrong with my Daddy?" That was a horrible moment and reminded me I needed to be careful. My rules were: Don't get up too quickly, don't carry too much, don't do too much, otherwise I could be out like a light. Despite it all, I wouldn't say I was feeling sorry for myself. I was willing to go through anything to reach the end goal. But I don't think I would be human not to have thought at some stage: 'What more do I have to go through here?' My body was in tatters.

I could have died after contracting sepsis, then I lost my eyesight and now I couldn't even go to the toilet normally without agonising pain. Weirdly, though, I still felt able to accept it. It was like: 'It is what it is', accept the pain, and eventually, one day soon, it will go. I remember talking to my doctor, Adrian, about it all and he said the only way it would heal would be to stop the treatment. There was not a chance that was going to happen. I told him I would accept all the pain as long as the treatment was going well, as long as I was continuing that journey towards the end goal.

If the chemotherapy is working against the disease, I will go through the pain because, in the long run, I am getting better. That is how I dealt with it all in the end. I got myself into war mode: I will take any pain you can throw at me – whatever it is, some foot pain, anywhere else, anything, I will take it. Bring it on! And if there are to be any scars from this battle, then fine. I will carry them through with me.

There is no quit in me, as I have said, and I wasn't going to resist anything either. I would accept the pain from the side effects and the things I couldn't control because that was easier than fighting it. It wouldn't make the pain any less but I accepted that the pain was here and wasn't looking to move away any time soon. It was something I had to get through and work with because the greater good was me getting home to my family at the end of it all. I remember people coming to see me and saying I didn't look well. Sylvan Ebanks-Blake, for one. He noticed I wasn't feeling the best and was limping, so he asked what was wrong with me. "In among everything else, Sylv," I replied. "Where do you want me to start?"

It was while he was up seeing me early in the New Year that I received some other news which rocked me; something which had absolutely nothing to do with the illness. We were sat around chilling when we both received a text from the Wolves head of media Paul Berry saying that Fozzie – the long-serving club programme editor and historian John Hendley – had passed away. Foz was one of those characters, a lifelong Wolves fan, who had worked at the club for years, long before us, and would probably have been there for the rest of his days. We all loved him, all the players and all the staff. I remember looking at my phone and not quite believing the text, wondering if I was reading it right. It didn't sink in at all and, although I wasn't well at all, I had to phone Paul to find out what had happened and was told Foz had died suddenly, probably of a heart attack.

I was gutted, it couldn't sink in. Foz was 'my man' and one of those at the club I was really used to and comfortable with – we had a lot of banter. He did a players' quiz in the programme and it usually ended up as a bit of a disaster with certain lads accusing him of helping some and not others. I'd tell him he was prejudiced against me any time I lost, although I was rubbish, but everyone loved him. He was always ready for banter. If he was around now, I'd be making sure I was still in touch with him, hammering him. It is so sad he has gone.

It was even more difficult for me because I knew I wouldn't be able to go to the funeral. I knew Foz would understand the reasons why but, at the same time, it felt like I hadn't done him justice. I just knew I was too ill to be around people. Even now, I still feel like I haven't paid my respects and at some point, I will go and have a pint somewhere, maybe at his local, and dedicate it to him. He sure liked a drink, so that will be my way of saying goodbye and I am sure he will be somewhere, smiling down on me.

Foz wasn't the only Wolves stalwart to be lost around that time, with one of the club's former groundsmen Terry Carver passing away a few months later. Terry was another person I had known for a very long time, another character around the club, who would hammer me as a goalkeeper just like most groundsmen do! TC would always be telling me I was wrecking his pitch and I'd be telling him that the pitch wasn't good enough. There is generally that love/hate relationship between goalkeepers and groundsmen, although always with a lot of fun. I think they all love keepers because we are a bit loopy and are usually out for training first and will chat to them. But then they hate what we do to their beloved grass. There are always mini-squabbles about the goalmouth and the penalty area but it's always in jest. Terry was always on my case but he was a really top guy who will also be sadly missed.

And the great Cyrille Regis passed away just a couple of weeks after Foz in the January. I didn't know him too well but know all about him and knew he was an inspiration. He was like a mentor figure to a lot of younger players, including Morgan Gibbs White at Wolves, so we would see him around and he always looked so fit, as if he could still get out there and play. After his passing, I saw all the tributes and realised what he had actually achieved in his career and what he had been through in breaking down barriers off the pitch. What he had done for black players, black people, ethnic communities, is a legacy which I don't think will ever be forgotten.

So that news about Foz, Terry and Cyrille came at a time when I was really struggling with the side effects of what I was going through. It was a tough period, physically and mentally, because I'd been building up to this period of treatment and thinking it would be the home straight. But when I came to it, with all the problems, it definitely didn't feel like I was approaching the finish line. I wondered if it was ever going to end. It was definitely challenging me in every sense. Yes, I could see the light at the end of the tunnel but it still felt as though it was only going to be baby steps that would take me there.

20

Eagles flying high

Going back into the Championship with Wolves for the 2014/15 season was also all about trying to take steps forward. And we made a very good start, winning four of the first five League games and proving very hard to beat. I think we had only lost a couple of League games going into November but then, as seemed to happen quite a lot, we had a really bad month. We lost five in a row before getting back to some form and we weren't too far away from the play-off picture going into the New Year.

Tomasz Kuszczak had been signed but I kept my place until I picked up a hip injury at Bolton at the end of January and didn't come back until April. When I did return, the team were flying. Benik Afobe, Bakary Sako and Nouha Dicko were in exciting form up top and I got back in for a victory at Nottingham Forest and then a great 4-3 win against Leeds in which Dave Edwards scored a late winner. Molineux was absolutely rocking that day and the points took us into the play-off places, looking all the world like we had the momentum to keep it going.

Then we went to play Blues at St Andrew's and took the lead but they quickly equalised and then Demarai Gray scored the winner in the second half. That defeat finished us to be honest. I remember coming off the pitch feeling gutted. Because of the rivalry between Wolves and Blues, St Andrew's was a place I really loved to play. Coming from Birmingham and knowing a lot of Blues fans, I found added spice to those games and that made it even harder to swallow on that day. You could feel it from their team and in their stadium that they knew they had put a massive dent in our hopes. And so it proved.

We lost our next game at Middlesbrough and only drew at home to Ipswich then I had a minor knee injury which ruled me out against Wigan and Millwall.

Although we won both of those games with Tomasz in goal, it wasn't enough. Despite picking up a good total of 78 points, we missed out on the play-offs on goal difference. For so long, it looked like we might get there given that fantastic run and it somehow seemed as if it might happen as the club's former owner and great benefactor Sir Jack Hayward had passed away half-way through the season. The day he died, we played an FA Cup replay against Fulham at Molineux when the snow came down in extra-time. But the tributes which came at our next game against Blackpool were incredible.

Wolverhampton is an industrious sort of town where people work hard and the football club is in the heart of that community. Sir Jack arrived in 1990 and pumped some money in to give people hope and that meant a lot to so many. So while he is someone I wasn't necessarily around all that much, I was well aware of his influence and, when I met him, I knew I was talking to someone who had been such a key part of Wolves' recent history.

Looking back now, from a football point of view, it never quite took off from just missing out on the play-offs and, the following season, which proved to be Kenny Jackett's last at the club, was very different. Bakary had left, Nouha got injured and then Richard Stearman left as well. Things seemed to become far more pragmatic all of a sudden. Instead of pushing on from winning the League One title and gone so close to reaching the play-offs, it seemed to become more a case of struggling to stay afloat in the division.

Steve Morgan put the club up for sale and was looking for a new investor, so the budget was reduced in terms of transfers and we lost some of our best players. We had to turn into more of a solid team, trying to grind out results rather than producing the exciting football we had over the second half of the previous season. It was to prove a difficult time and I count myself in that as well, as young Arsenal keeper Emi Martinez came in on loan and I was dropped. I had struggled a bit during pre-season, suffering from niggling knee injuries, and I didn't play too much in the friendlies. I think I maybe only played one full 90 minutes, then we were at Blackburn on the first day of the season. I made a hash of their goal and could have done better with it but I still felt sharp enough and we went on to win the game. For me, my general performance was good despite my error. I wouldn't say it was a complete howler either, but just the sort of mistake goalkeepers make from time to time.

As all us keepers know, strikers or midfielders make a mistake and often not much gets said but if we drop one, then more often than not it's a goal. If I was missing anything, it was maybe that extra bit of sharpness from playing in matches as it had been a few months since I had been in regular action but the only way to build that up again is by playing more matches. I went into training the day after Blackburn to be told I was being dropped and that Emi was going to be the first choice. Now,he is a good goalkeeper and a really good guy as well. But he was fairly young and inexperienced, although I suppose that is why he was moving from Arsenal to Wolves, to try to gain that experience.

Kenny called me to his office to break the news and, because I really hadn't seen it coming, I didn't have too much to say in response. The only way I can describe it is to say it felt like my girlfriend had just dumped me. To be honest, it really hurt. That was followed by anger and probably thinking Kenny was an arsehole just at that point in time! Maybe it was the timing of it all as well, coming straight after the first League game, which we had won after all.

I think the changing room was shocked and the fans were shocked – I felt I had done well for the club over two or three seasons and the supporters felt that, too. The decision also put pressure on Emi as well, right from the start. Most of the time, as a goalkeeper on loan, you are there to replace someone who has been injured, not to replace the first choice who has suddenly been told he is not going to be playing. If I had carried on making mistakes for the next few games, I could have understood it better. But, after one game, when I had made a little error but was otherwise looking sharp, I didn't think it was a situation that needed such drastic action.

I made my feelings known to Kenny the next day but would never rock the boat and, like all goalkeepers when they are not playing, I carried on training just as hard and supporting Emi as much as I could. As it was, I was back in after a couple of games but by then it had become a tricky one to deal with. It was at the back of my mind that I might be dropped again if I made a mistake and that thought left me feeling like I was not on top of my game.

Being a goalkeeper is so much to do with the mind that you don't need any form of doubt when you are out on the pitch. Without wishing to blame others – because of course ultimately it came down to me – I was now in doubt about my position at the club. That crept into my game and that slight bit of doubt would affect my movement, decision-making and communication, and that was a recipe for mistakes. So, sure enough, I didn't play to my best and was dropped again, Emi being restored to the team.

But he was injured in early November, just as I was called up for Nigeria for the first time. That call-up gave me a big boost coming when it did and when I went back into Wolves' side, with Emi injured, I kept my place for the rest of the season. When he was fit again, Emi was on the substitutes' bench and I have to say he was – still is – a top keeper. I didn't feel any personal satisfaction in seeing off his challenge for the shirt but I was definitely watching him in training and thinking: 'You are good, man! You're probably better than me but just need more experience.'

As the season went on, it proved to be one in which very little else happened. We had the chance to play at Upton Park in the FA Cup and pushed West Ham close before losing 1-0. That tie came after we really needed to grind out some results but it wasn't the most exciting time for all the reasons I've given about the club seemingly scaling back and waiting for a buyer. We finished in the middle of the table and I think the fans were all a bit disillusioned by that time, waiting to see what happened next. And what did happen next was the takeover by Fosun.

As players, you don't tend to hear too much about matters like that higher up the club and you end up, just like the fans, looking at all the speculation and picking up information wherever you can. But it was when we were coming back from pre-season in Ireland that news broke about the takeover and it seemed that Kenny would be replaced. For me, that was sad because I really enjoyed working with him, although he had dropped me the previous season. I still believe I played some of my best football when Kenny was in charge.

Fosun apparently missed out on their first target in Julen Lopetegui but then brought in top former Italian keeper in Walter Zenga. Ultimately, it was to prove another difficult time for the club and Walter only lasted three months or so, but I got on with him very well. His mentality was very different to other managers and his training methods were very unfamiliar as well. I'm not sure we had a day off throughout that three months!

A bit like Stale Solbakken, Walter was coming into a new league and it was going to take him time to adjust. I don't think he quite 'got' the Championship straightaway. There were more new players coming in as well and a combination of all that, with the players still at the club and others being pushed out, made for a turbulent time as the owners tried to find their feet.

In that situation, when results don't go your way, it is a recipe for the atmosphere not to be great in the changing room and we had started to struggle by the time Walter left. Yet we started well and also had some good results, with good football to match at times. We won the big local derby at Blues, then produced a great performance to win at Newcastle. It was just that again we didn't maybe have that grit and collective determination that any squad needs to succeed on a consistent basis in the Championship. Although we had some good wins, we also had some really poor defeats and I remember being thumped at home by Barnsley on a Tuesday night. Our shape had completely gone and we conceded all four goals in the last 20 minutes.

There was a lot of change at the club in a very short space of time, with player movement as well, and it was all very chaotic. Ultimately, it wasn't long before Walter moved on but I got on well with him and Andrea Butti, who came in as a team manager, sorting everything out behind the scenes. Even if it didn't work and it was very different, it was also quite exciting; something new which maybe we'd not had at Wolves before. It was certainly lively as they were very loud and outgoing as people, and very open. They were passionate characters and were more than happy to show their range of emotions.

Coming after Kenny, who was far more measured and subdued, it was certainly a contrast and something I hadn't experienced with a manager before. I enjoyed some aspects of it all but could see why it didn't work out in the end. Walter was vocal, fiery and animated in the dressing room. He had a different philosophy, coming over from Italy, and had been at a lot of clubs. Whoever came in was going to find it difficult with so many different changes under the new owners, and a fair bit of instability off the back of what had been a very stable time under Kenny. It was hard for everything and everyone to gel, so perhaps it was no surprise that Walter wasn't about for long.

Things soon improved again when Paul Lambert arrived as head coach. I have to say I loved working with him and really enjoyed the time he was at the club. He was a 'man's man' and you could go in his office and have a proper adult conversation without any fear of being judged or having anything held against you. He came into a difficult situation with the way we had started the season and all the player changes but he quickly got a reaction. As long as the lads gave him everything, he didn't mind and he would take the hit for anything and back us 100 per cent.

It could have ended up as another disaster of a season and we may even have been relegated again. But Paul's arrival helped steady the ship and made sure we maintained our Championship status, which proved a springboard for what was to follow. I remember at one point during that season, Jeff Shi, the new chairman, pulled all the players in. And he was really calm. It surprised me a little because I thought Fosun might be concerned at how things were going in their first season but he was fine and just told everyone not to panic. He said there was no pressure, that the owners knew where they wanted to go and that they would get there however long it took. If a season had to be sacrificed in pursuit of the long-term aims, so be it – their overall plans for the club were not going to change.

I remember thinking at the time that it's not often you get that sort of speech from the chairman. Usually, it is the complete opposite. Jeff gave the players his backing and told us that anything we needed, just to let him know. He didn't want anyone to play with fear, they had a long-term vision and we just had to go out and play. He was always around the training ground, which is another thing you don't often see, but he was there just to show his support and also get a handle on how the club was run.

Paul managed to stabilise things but we still found ourselves in a bit of trouble. I had missed the great FA Cup win at Liverpool, thanks to being sent off at Norwich the week before, but I played in the game against Chelsea, which was a great atmosphere, but came as one of six consecutive defeats. We ground out a fairly dull win at home to Rotherham to end our long run without a win, then had two away games against Brentford and Fulham, and won both. How little did I know about how my life was going to change after that appearance at Fulham!

I could never have imagined they would be my last two games for Wolves, even more so my last two games in football. Craven Cottage was a stadium I always associated with us doing well at and getting good results. We went 2-0 up before Fulham pulled one back, then Dave Edwards grabbed a third which sealed the win. We always felt we had enough to stay in the Championship but you have to go out and prove it. With those two away wins, it felt like we had pulled away from danger.

As I came off the pitch that Saturday afternoon in the March of 2017, never could I have thought that would be it for me and competitive football. I had been struggling with my hamstring for a while, probably for a lot of that season, although it was never serious enough to really keep me out. It was only after the Fulham game that the problem became clear. I stayed down in London and had a night out with Kevin McDonald, our former midfielder who had moved on to Fulham. I hadn't seen him for a while and was meeting up with the Nigeria squad in London on the following Monday, so it worked out well to stay in the capital.

It was a big result for Wolves and it's fair to say I had a few drinks that night to celebrate. The hamstring felt a bit sore that evening, and even more so when I woke up the next morning. I probably didn't say anything when I reported to meet the squad – that was me sometimes. I never wanted to not be able to train or play. We were training at Barnet and I started to do the warm-up but something wasn't right. I was struggling to move properly,so the physio did some tests and discovered I had a tear.

The problem was that some of the Nigeria squad were struggling to get over to England because of VISA issues and I was the only keeper who had made it so far. There was a friendly coming up on the Thursday night at Barnet against Senegal and there was a fair bit of pressure on me to be available. The Nigerian physio still wanted me to play but obviously I was talking to Wolves head of medical Phil Hayward and we shared a very different opinion. Thankfully, the other keeper arrived the night before the game, so I didn't need to be involved.

I stayed with the squad and watched the game before getting back to Wolves in what was still the international break. I saw a specialist and started my rehab, with not much of the season left. We were pretty much safe by then and I was more worried about trying to be fit and ready for pre-season than getting back during the current one. I was also thinking about the schedule and how things would fall in terms of going away for pre-season, especially with Maya being due over the summer. We managed to go away for a couple of weeks, then I was back in for most of the summer, going in for rehab work and working in the gym with Matty Murray.

Having missed out on that Nigeria game, I was also keen to get playing for my country again. That international recognition, coming so late in my career, had been a massive source of celebration and brought me some of the biggest and best moments of my footballing life.

Where do you start when it comes to those incredible times I enjoyed with Nigeria? At the very beginning, I suppose. I qualified through my dad, who was born there, and first had a mention way back in 2007 when Berti Vogts was in charge. Maybe he had seen a list of Nigerian-qualified players and was trying to get everyone together. He had picked a 37-man provisional squad for an African Cup of Nations qualifier with Uganda and myself and Gabby Agbonlahor had been included for the first time. I was injured and unfortunately couldn't make it. Who would have imagined it would be eight years before I had another chance? When the call-up came, I had just been dropped at Wolves when Emi had come in. To think that some people might not accept football being a strange game!

Vincent Enyeama was the undisputed top goalkeeper for Nigeria and had been for so many years. He was also the captain, so it was always going to be difficult to dislodge him. I still felt that maybe I might have had an opportunity and been involved at some stage, even just as part of the squad as cover or if Vincent wasn't available. Timing is everything I suppose and it was nice to get the call when it eventually arrived, especially as I'd just been dropped at Wolves. The one advantage of the call-up coming a few years later was that, at the age of 29, I was ready for it and could deal with it. When I did get in, I found myself playing straightaway and was mentally up to it, which I may not have been eight years earlier with far less experience under my belt. Of course I was still nervous, still had some jitters, that is normal, but I was more of a man by then and had played a lot more club games. I was prepared to step up to that level. As soon as I got into training and came up against some top players, I knew I was ready,

Although born in England, I had had a really deep connection with the Nigerian side of my family since I was a kid. I would regularly visit them in London and they would visit us in Birmingham. I was really strong with that side of my family, so to be picked for Nigeria meant a huge amount to all of us – it was never going to be a second choice or just a matter of convenience. Everyone assumes that had I ever been good enough to be picked for England, then it would have been great. Well, obviously, it would, but there is no way it would have meant any more to me than being picked for Nigeria. It actually felt more empowering for me to be selected for Nigeria. I was massively proud and the sense of pride everyone has for football over there made the whole thing feel right.

It made me feel even closer to the country and, as well as the football side, it gave me the chance to travel back there again much more than I would otherwise have been able to. I had been a few times but this meant I could potentially be going a couple of times a year. And the amount of pride my family had in me being called up for Nigeria...that made it even more special. When the phone call came, from the manager Sunday Oliseh, I thought it was a wind-up to be honest! I assumed it was one of my friends or cousins just messing about. The call had come a while before the squad was announced and he was just chatting to me and asking about my feelings and whether I would be interested. Would I be interested? Yes. Absolutely!

I think he was checking how I felt about my affiliation and seeing how keen I was, as obviously he didn't know me at all previously or know anything about my life. I told him I would definitely want to play for him and definitely want to play for Nigeria. He said he would take it into consideration as he thought about his next squad and, before I knew it, I was in. There were two fixtures to play, an African Cup of Nations qualifier in Tanzania and a friendly at home to Niger. I remember meeting up with the squad and having a few days training. It was tough with the heat as it was something I hadn't been used to in England. Obviously!

There had been a lot of talk about whether Vincent would be able to meet up with the squad. He had been the Nigerian keeper for 12 years but his mother had passed away, so it was understandably unlikely he was going to join up. All of a sudden, from travelling over thinking I was going to be part of the squad, I was about to start a qualifier in the African Cup of Nations on my debut. Things move fast in football. In my head, I suppose I had been preparing to enjoy being part of a squad, getting to know the lads, training well, and then maybe getting a few minutes in the friendly. Oh no, it was the complete opposite. I was starting the big qualifier in Tanzania.

Sometimes, opportunities arrive in football and in life, that you don't expect, but you have to make the most of them. And so it was that day in Tanzania, when I kept a clean sheet and ended up being named Man of the Match. It was a really tough game in blistering heat and we came away with a 0-0 draw. It was an amazing experience, the stadium was full, and singing the national anthem was an incredible moment for me. I had known the anthem in terms of the tune but not the words and that was something I made sure I learned before the game. I wanted to be a part of it and not stand there without being able to sing. It is quite a short anthem and I already knew the ring to it, which helped. But I had already been part of a load of singing on the coach on the way to the game.

I remember feeling a bit nervous as I got on the bus to go to the ground. But everyone just started singing on the journey and that settled me down straightaway. If none of the other players were nervous and were relaxed enough to have a good old sing-song, there was nothing for me to worry about. Any nervous tension in my head was very quickly gone.

It certainly wasn't any lack of seriousness about the game – everyone was really motivated and fired up for what was to come. But it just created a really good atmosphere and showed the spirit within the squad.

There were a lot of holy songs, songs about God, all part of the Nigerian culture, and it gave me a real sense of belief. We also held a prayer meeting the night before the game and prayed before and after every training session. There were Christians, Catholics and Muslims in the squad, all praying together, 20 or so people, and I found that really powerful. It fitted in with how I was feeling at that stage of my life, in terms of my belief system, and I felt the power of energy and spirit and holiness. I wouldn't say I am massively into one religion or another but I believe in spirits and energy. The praying and singing felt really powerful in my soul and made me comfortable and, as a newcomer to the squad, it made me feel part of the group. There was something really powerful about us all being together praying, a collective feeling, which increased my inner belief. To see Christians and Muslims praying together, it's kind of a really positive advert for the world, isn't it? There were people speaking in Arabic as well and we would all sit together and pray – it was very powerful.

The way the game went solidified the thought that I was good enough to play international football. I loved every minute of it. Dad was very proud of me being able to make my debut for Nigeria, in fact my whole family were immensely proud. A lot of my family still live over there and to see me appearing on their TV news made them super happy! Dad wasn't able to get over for the Tanzania game but he did make it for the friendly which followed against Niger, which we won 2-0. That made it such a special memory for me. He always talked about someone from Onitsha, the village he was from, becoming the first person to represent Nigeria, and now that was me. People over there that will have known my dad...this was now a legacy that people could follow. That was so important for me, way more important than anything the international breakthrough had done for my own profile. To know that Dad and some of my aunties saw my second appearance and that win over Niger was something else.

I think playing for my country made me more proud in terms of what it meant for my family than my own pride in the achievement. Even my mum was so proud, even though she isn't Nigerian. That was the biggest thing for me, making my family happy, along with trying to make a nation proud as well. My grandad was no longer alive and I remember thinking what it would have meant to him to know I had played for Nigeria. Ahead of the Tanzania game, I was quite emotional during the national anthem and looked up to the sky, wishing he was there to see it. He had come over to England from Nigeria and I had been very close to him when I was growing up.

Aside from my family, the support and love of the Nigerian people towards me was off the scale. It was a bit like the Wolves situation towards the end, with Nigeria fans giving me the same sort of love the Wolves fans did. That level of support is strange for a player to receive from any club and not many are lucky enough to have that sort of relationship. I had it twice, with Wolves and Nigeria, and that is something I would never ever take for granted.

As soon as I went there, it was just pure love. Anywhere I turned up, people made a fuss of me, whether it was my team-mates, the coaching staff or the players. I felt like I fitted in straightaway. With football in Nigeria, it was the same kind of situation as it is for English players in this country. You can't go anywhere without being recognised. If you go through the airport, people know you. Check into a hotel, people know you. There is a lot of attention. Everywhere I went, people would be saying to me: "Number one, number one" and that brought an energy to me.

The Nigerian people love football so much and they watch all the games. When we were staying in hotels before games, there were fans outside all of the time – I'm not sure they even went home! There was proper love everywhere and they always wished us well when we were getting on and off the coaches or going out to play. I remember one day after a game in Abuja, when a lot of the players had gone. There was one time previously when I had got straight on a plane after a game to come back to Wolverhampton, so I would arrive late on Thursday evening before a Saturday fixture. Then I ended up cramping up in a game against Ipswich, which wasn't great. So, on this occasion, I decided to stay on and spend the day in the hotel recovering and relaxing. I just popped out for a walk to the shop and all the fans were still there – I was wandering along chatting to them all and it was a great experience.

I was at that stage of my career where I was able to deal with all the attention and everything else so much easier, particularly in stepping into the shoes of a legend such as Vincent. He was an absolute hero and a hero for me – I loved him and loved watching him play. With what happened to his mother, he took the decision to retire and I suppose that came at the right time for both of us. He had played a lot of games and decided the time was right to finish and that gave me, even when I was perhaps heading into the latter stages of my career, a chance I had always wanted. I felt man enough to take it on, to follow in such illustrious footsteps, and I made sure I dismissed any media talk about it being Vincent against me, or making comparisons between the two of us. I told people I just wanted to play for Nigeria, and suggested they should not mention Vincent's name in relation to me because he is a legend and he's a legend to me as well!

I was never ever going to get close to playing the number of games for Nigeria that he did, or becoming the sort of legendary figure he did. But it had come at the right time for me, at a time – even though I had just been dropped at Wolves – when I was really enjoying my football. I made my international breakthrough but I knew it wouldn't last for ever, so I had to do everything I could to make sure I savoured the whole experience. It had taken so much hard work and determination to get there, I now had a far different perspective on life as well as football and was able to make sure I made the most of this incredible opportunity. I wasn't taking anything for granted and had more thoughtfulness at that stage of my career where I wasn't thinking about myself or my profile, more about enjoying what had come along and making sure I gave of my best.

It was certainly a very different set-up to what I had become used to at English clubs. The facilities, including the pitches, weren't as good, which was no surprise when you consider the different weather, the soil and several other factors. Sometimes, the Nigerian set-up could be a bit disorganised but everyone knew that and it was almost part of the fun. I have said before that I am someone who really likes structure and things to be planned but, when I was with Nigeria, it felt right just to go with it and enjoy it.

We'd wake up and not really know if we were travelling that day but we'd all just go with the flow. It was like the collective thought of: 'This is Nigeria, we do our best and everyone will make the most of what we have'. It wasn't like a European country where everything is laid on for you and there were always issues around the government and the Nigerian FA. But our approach was not to worry about it, and go with it, because if you worried about every little thing, you'd be moaning all the time. A bit like we all did at our clubs if things weren't spot on!

It certainly hasn't done Nigeria any harm in recent years and I think it helped the spirit and togetherness in the squad that maybe at times we were all mucking in together. After that first call-up and the two appearances, and with Vincent's retirement, I became the first-choice keeper for Nigeria and would go on to make ten appearances in total. Ten appearances that I will remember for the rest of my days, with a huge smile on my face. We didn't qualify for the African Cup of Nations, which is always disappointing, but we did produce some good results. We beat Cameroon 3-0, beat Mali, won in Zambia and drew with Egypt.

Above: A proud end-of-season walk with Mila, although she wasn't too keen to wave. Right: A victory over Villa was bound to have extra significance for Paul Lambert and yours truly. Below: Having both Danny Batth and Richard Stearman in front of me was a pleasure and here we are celebrating a big win.

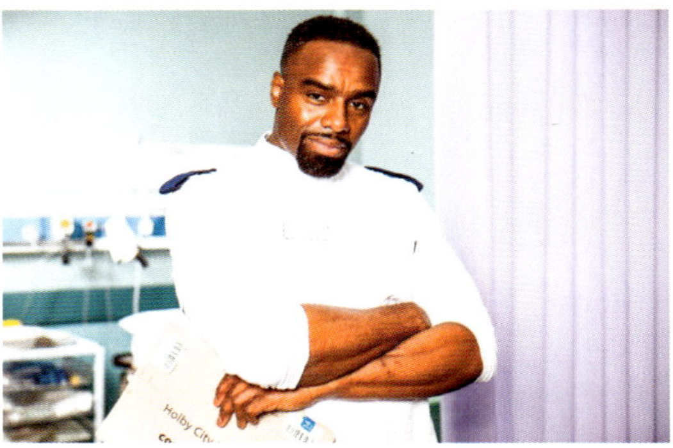

Top: Coady to the left of me, Dad to the right. I had paternal support at all games. Above left: My highly talented actor cousin, Charles 'Chucky' Venn, who provided the foreword for this book. Above: Looking on at a 2016 pre-season game in Cork. Left: Creating a pathway in international football.....

On tour with the Super Eagles

Representing Nigeria towards the end of my career was an incredible experience, for so many reasons.

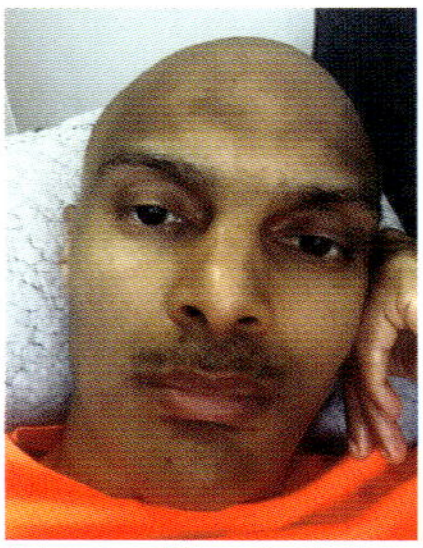

From having a ball with Nigeria, life in a hospital bed had its glum moments but that wonderful support from my team-mates and the Molineux fans always lifted my spirits. Above: Telford Wolves fly the flag at the England v Nigeria game at Wembley while, below, I was touched by this scene at the first game of 2017/18.

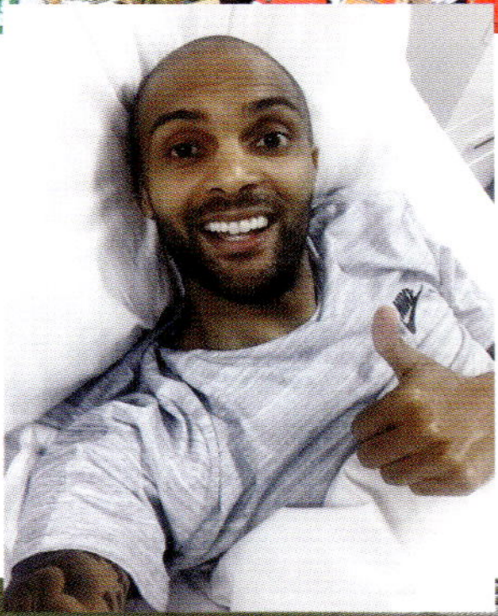

Above: Our first picture as a family of four! It was an incredible feeling to finally get to meet Maya. I will forever feel blessed with my beautiful girls and, happily, we could still enjoy the occasional play-time in hospital.

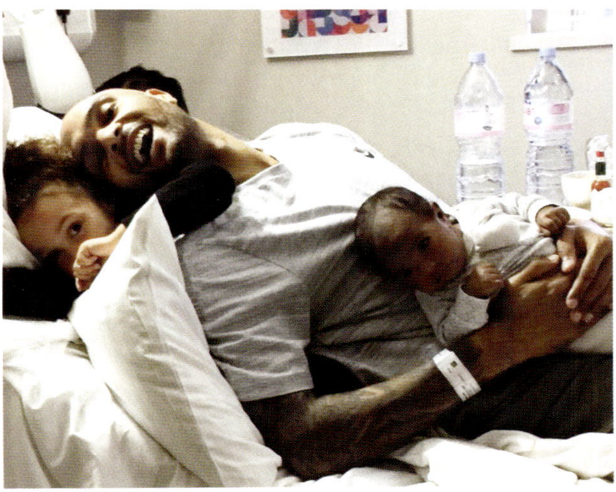

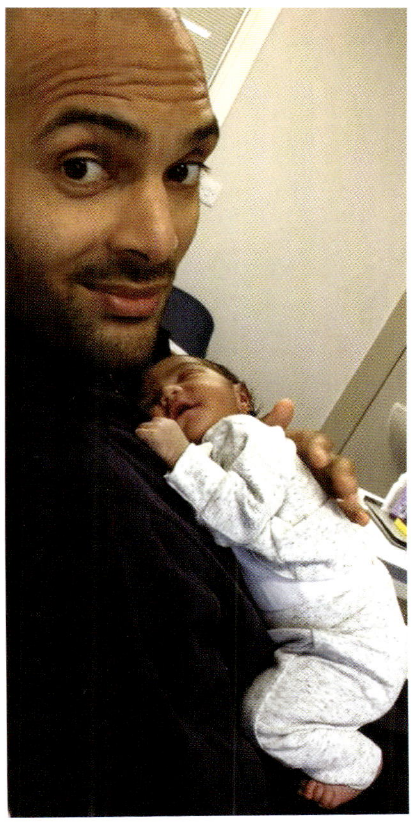

The long road to recovery would have felt longer and harder still had it not been for the welcome stream of visitors. How they helped when I most needed it!

Above left: With Joe Hart, who came to see me with my great friend Matty Murray at the start of my treatment.

Above: Dad on one side and, on the other, Stiliyan Petrov, who gave me a wonderful boost by dropping in to see me early on.

And left: Arm in arm with the skipper, another top mate.

Below: Going back to the training ground for the first time was strange but I had great support on announcing my retirement.

A trio of post-treatment treats....
Above: Carrying out the FA Cup fourth-round draw with the BBC's Mark Chapman and Robbie Keane at Molineux straight after Wolves' win over Liverpool.
Left: I still love a challenge - and riding 100 miles in the 2019 Velo was a big achievement. Image courtesy of SussexSportPhotography.
Below: Going 'home' and walking on to the pitch before Wolves' draw with Manchester City early in 2018/19. Keeping me company are Mila and my Godson, Shaya.

Above: I always enjoy fans' q&a nights, especially 'rinsing' Matty when he is hosting. Below: With Saba at a charity event – she has shown incredible strength. Right: With Maya, our very own miracle.

That draw with Egypt, when Mo Salah scored their goal in added time, was the maddest experience I have had in a stadium in my entire life! When we reached the stadium in Kaduna two hours before the game, it was already full, with both sets of fans. I had been really ill during the build-up and shouldn't really have played. I had never really been ill – up until then anyway – but I had really bad sickness and diarrhoea and hadn't eaten for two days. Excuse the phrase but I felt like I was on my deathbed, although little did I know that little treat was to come along just over a year later. I was feeling rough but the manager told me he really needed me to play. I don't think he was massively comfortable with the sub keeper at that time and wanted me out there in such an important game. I told him I would do my best and started drinking as much water as I could.

The heat, wow, it must have been 35 degrees for the game, and all I could eat was half a piece of dry bread not long before kick-off. Even going out to warm up in front of a full stadium, they were having to sit people on the racetrack around the pitch, just to get everyone in, and this was still an hour before the game. By the time we started, there were people up on the floodlights and all sorts – I think health and safety must have had a day off! It was a 25,000-capacity stadium, so they said, but there must have been double that many inside and I was shouting to my defenders and knew there was no way they were going to be able to hear me. It was incredible and a great experience, even though I was feeling absolutely dreadful.

I don't know how I got through the game to be honest and it was as bad as I have ever felt on a football pitch, even when compared to getting studded in my private regions on my debut at Aldershot. I did get through, somehow, but we were disappointed with the result and more so when we didn't go on to qualify. I ended up in hospital and on a drip before I was able to fly home. I wasn't well for a few days. I don't know whether it was food poisoning or what but I lost a stone very quickly.

I mention that game and party atmosphere and there was a different element to playing for Nigeria than for other teams, as the fans wanted to see attacking football and flair above anything else, maybe even results. You would hear a huge cheer every time Alex Iwobi put it through someone's legs, or there was a trick from Victor Moses, or something special from John Obi Mikel or Wilfred Ndidi. The crowd loved it and a wicked atmosphere built. It was also a very different atmosphere to English football and the English culture around stadiums.

Grounds in England become quite tense and aggressive with both sets of fans in there and, don't get me wrong, I love that and the atmosphere that it brings. I think as players you always thrive off that sort of intimidation and lively rivalries. But the pressure in Nigeria was not so much about the vibe between the fans, just that most of the people inside the stadium had just come along to see some flair. Sitting back and being all tactical and defensive? If you did that, you were going to get booed.

There was never really any crowd trouble either despite the big attendances and spectators ending up watching from anywhere that they could. In fact, the only trouble – if you could call it that – was usually trying to get away from the stadium after games because there were still so many fans around. We always had to have an armed escort to and from matches, usually from the Army, because people would take it on themselves to try to climb any barriers to get to us, not to cause any aggro, just to say hello. Nigeria can be a dangerous country, especially in certain regions, but my experience in seeing so many thousands of fans when we were getting to matches was wonderful – there was so much love. Yes, we would need an escort but that was just down to extreme excitement and I can't even remember seeing a scuffle let alone anything more serious.

Overall, my Nigeria time went well and I kept six clean sheets in those games. My last appearance came in the first qualifier for the 2018 World Cup, in Zambia in September, 2016. It was another lively experience and the President of Zambia came on the pitch before the game as the special guest to shake hands with all the players. I don't know what the political situation was in Zambia at the time but how mad to think that here was a young lad from the inner cities of Birmingham shaking hands with the President of Zambia in front of 50,000 people. Yes. I'd come a long way from those early days kicking a ball around on the streets outside our flat.

We were going into the Lion's Den that day. We hadn't won away for two years and it was the first qualifying game for the World Cup, so the pressure was on and expectation was high. We were under so much pressure at times but came away with a 2-1 win, which was a really great feeling. There was only a small pocket of Nigerian fans inside the stadium and I pulled off some good saves, which is always nice. To make a contribution like that and get off to a winning start in the qualification campaign was a decent way for me to finish, even though I wasn't to know at the time that I would never represent my country again.

I always felt we would have enough to get to the World Cup, even if sadly it was not meant to be in terms of my own involvement. Even before the Zambia game, I remember looking around the squad and thinking there was more than enough quality in there to make it to Russia. We had a defence that was working well together, with William Troost-Ekong and Leon Balogun, and the three of us had a really good relationship on and off the pitch. In midfield, we had the likes of Mikel and Ndidi, and then Iwobi, Moses and Odion Ighalo going forward – we were too good not to make it. Little did I know at that stage that I was destined not to play any part.

21

"Things are good"

If I had to wait a long time to play for Nigeria, it felt like nothing compared with the delay in my treatment during the most intense phase which followed the sepsis. What was supposed to be a six-week process ended up being 12, because once again my blood counts weren't moving. I had my bone marrow taken at the time because nothing was happening and it was worrying waiting for the results to see if the cancer had come back. No matter how positive a mindset I was in and how determined I was to avoid worrying about things I couldn't control, when I was going into hospital twice a week hoping for the bloods to improve and they didn't, it was tough.

It is difficult to properly explain that feeling of disappointment when you are so desperate to carry on with the treatment and you feel good, but the tests show you are not ready. I would wait around for hours thinking or trying to convince myself that today was going to be the day. That is when you do start to wonder whether something is going wrong. After five or six weeks, the decision was taken to take the bone marrow, which isn't the most pleasant experience as anyone who has gone through it will know.

It had been a very difficult winter, with the sepsis, the eye trouble, struggling to go to the toilet, then my blood counts not moving. The different complications had delayed everything and here I was in February and still a long way off completing the treatment. At the start of the process, I had targeted February as a time for completion and hopefully being in remission but I was nowhere near. I was also starting to miss home quite a bit by this stage. I had been back for a few days here and there but that wasn't the same and I was obviously missing my daughters hugely. Being in Manchester while I was waiting was making me a bit agitated as I felt I was missing out on a lot of simple things, like hearing my kids playing and waking up in the morning to all that activity of a family household.

Eventually, the bone marrow, which would have shown if there were any problems, came back clear. That was good news, and the doctor, Adrian, was brilliant with me over this period. He knew and understood how I was feeling with all the delays and it was just a case that my bone marrow was sensitive and took a bit longer to come back to normal than anyone else.

As I continued the treatment, often at times injecting myself with the chemotherapy at home and taking the tablets, it was a relief to get through that intense phase. A relief, also, that it left me needing to undergo only another couple of treatments. The new aim for completing everything was June and, despite all of the problems, it started to feel very close. The problem with my backside had become more manageable and it felt like I was over the worst of that pain, and my eyesight was coming back, so I could start reading again. I was also getting near to the end of the lease on my apartment, so it all felt like I was close to coming home – and that this was going to be an important time for me.

Those following two treatments went very smoothly, certainly compared with what had gone before. After the bone marrow had come back clear, I think it had all been agreed that it just took my bloods a bit longer to recover than some other patients. It gave everyone a boost that things were still moving in the right way. The medical people were staying positive and my bloods then reacted well over the final two treatment cycles.

I had tried to get to grips with everything to do with leukaemia while I was being treated, to understand more about the disease. Eight or months down the line, I had started to understand what the medics were looking at and the sort of markers they were looking for. I still needed some blood and platelet transfusions over those last two treatments and was in hospital on a couple of occasions after running a temperature. But, by now, I knew what to do and was able to accept anything that was associated with the treatment and the side effects it was giving me. I suppose I had become something of an expert towards the end of the process and wish I had possessed that knowledge and understanding when I was diagnosed but I'm not sure that is possible when everything is so new and you don't completely know what is going on.

In those early days, always in the back of my mind was the worries that the disease would later come back or that something I was feeling was going to cause me problems. As time went on, I learned to accept it all and not think about things too much, to accept that my body had been through quite an ordeal and would never be the same again. It was around the May of 2018, nearly a year after diagnosis, that I had my last main treatment. I remember finishing it all and starting to get ready to move out of the apartment in Manchester. The plan was to get back and be ready for Mila's birthday on June 10th. I'd move out of the apartment on the 6th and be back home for a few days before the big day.

It felt a bit surreal planning for it, as the treatment and everything associated with it had become the norm for me over such a long time. I was obviously happy to finally be getting out of Manchester – no offence Manchester! – and to be on my way home, although I knew I'd be going back to Christie's very soon afterwards for a check. I wasn't escaping that easily! And it certainly wasn't a huge celebratory moment to be out of there, because there was still a long way to go and there would be many more tests and potential further treatment to follow.

If I needed a reminder of that and the fact I wasn't going to be able to go straight back into normal life, it came with Mila's birthday. I was really happy to be there for it and she had some of her friends around for a party but, at the same time, I still wasn't well. I was okay but not well enough to be around too many people for too long. A few of our close friends came round with their kids and they went off to the Dessert Shop, where her main party was taking place. I was buzzing seeing Mila enjoying herself and being around friends again but I couldn't go out with them.

Kids pick up bugs all the time and I couldn't take that risk so soon after completing the treatment. My blood counts were still on the floor compared with when I was well and I was still very susceptible to catching illnesses. That was the last thing I needed having gone through so much and just started getting myself settled back home. I remember putting Mila to bed that night and being asked by her why I hadn't gone to her party. I tried to deflect the question, saying I was there in the background, but she was crying her eyes out. "I can't believe you didn't come to my birthday party," she sobbed. I didn't like lying to her by suggesting I was there but I didn't want her to feel like I didn't care either. It was all so difficult. She cried herself to sleep and, in a pretty bad year, that was something else that was right up there with the worst of my experiences. She didn't understand what was going on but it proper knocked me about.

I should have been so happy to be back home, sharing her big day with her, but I still couldn't do everything I wanted and was devastated she had noticed I wasn't there. I felt so guilty I had ruined her birthday and that was the first time I had cried in a very long time. She was distraught and it broke me, to be honest. It really hurt me to see her that upset. I had heard her cry many times before, of course I had, but not because she had been hurt by her dad. I remember thinking it was the worst feeling in the world and I never wanted to experience it again. It was very hard at times not being able to tell her the full truth about my condition and in particular not being able to tell her why I couldn't go to the party. Why I had let her down so much?

I wanted her to know I loved her and wanted her to understand how happy I was to be back at home for her birthday. It was tough to take and an indication of just what the disease had taken from me over the previous year. This was supposed to be a joyous occasion but was a painful reminder that the leukaemia was by no means over and done with. There were still more steps to take, more treatment to be had. I still had to take a lot of care with what I was doing. I wasn't yet ready to get back into normal life.

However positive I had been mentally and however strong I tried to stay, I had still gone through so much. I don't tend to look back and think about everything too much but, when I do, I still feel a kind of shiver. Sometimes, I don't think that person was me. It feels like I am talking about someone else and thinking about something else. I don't think I fully realise what I had gone through because at the time I was accepting the journey and just going day by day. I was concentrating on getting through everything that had been thrown at me. So, although I was obviously very happy to be home, it was difficult because I still wasn't right.

I still wasn't well but I was supposed to be really happy and so it was a strange mix of emotions. I knew I still had to go back to hospital, so, while I was buzzing to be home, there was still that sense that I wasn't okay. I was still under their care. It was nothing like a 'hurrah' moment of celebration, party time, I am recovered, and will never have to go for treatment again. It was just another stepping stone along what was a very long and difficult journey.

After a couple of weeks, I did indeed have to go back to Christie's to be checked out, so we decided to make a day of it. I sure know how to show Saba a good time, don't I? The four of us went up for the day, I was able to move around a bit, and we had some dinner in and around going to the hospital. My bloods had come back in good shape after the final treatment and I was having a conversation with Jo, one of the nurses. "What do I tell everyone?" I asked her.

"How do I describe where I am at now?" It felt like I needed a label of what I actually was, because I still felt in a grey area. I didn't think I had cancer anymore but I wasn't too sure if I was cured.

Having been back home, the better I felt, the more I would be getting out and about, maybe going to the shops and bumping into people I knew. When they asked how I was and how things were looking for the future, I had no idea what I should tell them. I needed that label, that explanation, to let people know how I was doing, that reassurance of what I could say. Jo told me I was in complete remission and that, yes, I still had further treatment to come, but I could live my life as normal. Everything was good and I was allowed to say it was good.

I'd always been nervous about saying things were going well, nervous of becoming too carried away. If you tell people things are going well, then they take a bad turn, you have to explain it all later and talk about what went wrong. Jo was great in passing on the information, just as the whole medical team had been fantastic with me throughout. The nurses at Christie's went above and beyond and I just couldn't pick any of them out above each other. I never used to ask for anything. Like I say, I wanted to try and crack on with everything myself if I could but they would always ask me and just make sure. "Do you want anything, Carl?" "Nah, I'm good thanks." I'm not fussy, I do just get on with things but, in the long run and especially when I was really struggling, they really came into their own. I didn't ask for much help but, when I did, they were brilliant.

They could always tell how I was feeling. It is why they are so fantastic at their jobs and each and every one of them did everything possible for me when I needed their help. I couldn't hide things after a while and they could tell when I wasn't great. "Come on, Carl," they would say. "Give us your bag." And the way they treated my family.....that was just amazing. They did everything they could for them as well and would answer all their questions and keep them up to speed on everything that was going on.

My doctor at Christie's, Adrian Bloor, was also very good, and would explain everything that was going on. He was so intelligent and professional, as you would expect in his line of work, but we had a really good relationship and I knew I could talk to him about anything. We'd talk about the illness and the treatment, then go off key and chat about holidays or something completely different. It helped and he was so thorough that I always felt I was in safe hands. In fact, I'd say the very best hands. Again, that was important for us all to know.

Saba, Mum and Dad had a lot of questions and Adrian and the medical staff were always available to answer them. They never gave out any false hope. It was always straight and honest but the whole family knew that they were doing absolutely everything they could to get me through it. We had that feeling right from the start, from those appointments with Manos Nikolousis, the consultant haematologist I saw in the early stages. Our world had fallen apart but Manos took control and his door was always open for us – as it still is. Like Adrian, he is so professional and also has a really friendly demeanour. He has time for people and cares what people are going through, and their families. He just settled all us down and made me feel like I meant something and wasn't just a number. We were fortunate to have people like that around just when we needed them most and Manos is very much a friend of the family now – we all love him!

So, with all that help and so much more, I had made that progress and had come home. It was a relief to know I was in complete remission and a relief to know what I could say to people. I didn't want them acting weird with me when they saw me if they didn't know what was happening and what my prospects were. And it was so funny, because I think the first person I saw back home after that, standing outside the tattoo shop near my house, was a Wolves fan. It just had to be, didn't it? You couldn't make it up. What a coincidence, or maybe everything does indeed happen for a reason?

Sure enough, he recognised me and came up to ask me how I was. Straightaway, I remembered it all from the conversation with Jo, just what she had said to me. I looked at him, took a deep breath, composed myself and smiled. "I'm in complete remission mate... things are good."

22

Back to civilisation

Back home again, it did take time to adapt back into normal life. Having had such a strange and difficult year, based mainly in Manchester and sometimes really struggling with the treatment, I was in different territory. I had only been getting home for a few days at a time but had now found out from the nurse how I should explain my situation. I was starting to see people around the more I went out and also decided to send a tweet, just to keep people updated. I never really wanted to be the centre and focus of people's attention but the support and well wishes I received were incredible and had really helped.

I certainly wasn't tweeting to get a reaction. I just wanted people to know so that, when I saw them again now I was back, they knew they could behave normally with me. There was no need to be worried or embarrassed about what they should say, and how I was doing, so we could all just crack on and have a conversation. But what followed from my tweet on June 23rd, 2018, was phenomenal. I really underestimated the response and the massive reaction to that tweet was really humbling and another sign of the support I had received.

I'd put the tweet out because I just wanted to be able to pop to Tesco's and have a normal conversation – instead, it ended up as a big item on the news! It was a sign of the love and affection which people had for me, which I massively appreciated, but I was still locked in a kind of unknown spell. Yes, I was in remission but would still be needing tests and treatment, although the best thing was being able to return to some sort of normality. I could go on a walk to the park in the morning, I could go out to eat, I could go and pick Mila up from school and I didn't need to be so paranoid about picking up an infection. Meeting her from school for the first time was something I was particularly looking forward to. I remember she was so excited to see me and just ran through the playground and jumped into my arms. I hugged her and kissed her cheek, and we walked back to the car holding hands. For the first time in such a long time, I was able to say: "How was your day?" I think even a few of the school moms who were there watching were welling up.

It was all about readjusting to a normal sort of life and that isn't as easy as it probably sounds. The only way I can explain it – and, trust me, I've not been in prison – but perhaps it is a bit like coming out of jail and getting back into civilisation. You see people come out of jail and you can tell they are not quite back there mentally and have to get used to being back around other people again, passing the time of day, having conversations, doing small talk. At times, Saba might suggest that we go out for breakfast and my instinctive response would be: "I'd love to but there will be too many people in there." Now, actually, I could go for breakfast and I could go to the park with the kids whereas for the previous 11 months, my instinctive first thought had always been no.

Even readjusting to being around people in crowds again, wow, that was strange! It felt quite uncomfortable for a time. There is so much bacteria out there, which I had never really thought about before I was ill. If someone shook my hand, although I know they were being friendly and supportive, I'd whip out the hand gel straight after. Sorry, everyone! If we went out to eat, I'd be looking to see if the place was clean or wondering whether the food had been cooked properly. I was desperate to avoid picking up something which would see me back in a hospital room – the sepsis had really opened my eyes to it all and brought home to me how important it was to be careful.

I'm not saying I never went outside through the time I was being treated – of course I did – but it was weird readjusting to it as normal again and spending more time in public situations. The worries about infections, meeting people and so on, I'm definitely over that now but, for a time, I found it strange. But still there wasn't any point taking any risks and I wasn't rushing into Birmingham and Wolverhampton to be among big crowds where there might be so many germs knocking about. I could have picked up a virus and, with the way my health was, it could have been enough to put me back in hospital for a week. Make no mistake, I'd spent enough time there over the previous year.

Things looked different to me when I came home as well. It's tricky to explain but people looked different than they used to and I was mentally having to get used to everything again. It was just another phase to get through, another step on the journey, and that included making plans to get away for a break as well;

something we hadn't been able to do for so long. My best friend was getting married, so we went to the wedding in Malaga and that was a really nice occasion which we enjoyed greatly.

Talking of weddings, I got around to proposing to Saba. I'd had this vision during my treatment, particularly through the tough times, of being well again, with Saba and the kids on holiday somewhere. Being able to go somewhere nice in the summer, the four of us, was always in the back of my mind as something I wanted to aim for. We were in Ibiza and had enjoyed a great day on the beach before walking back to the car. Mila told Saba that I wanted to ask her something, so I proposed and, thankfully, she said yes! Everything I had been through had been difficult for those around me to watch and deal with, no one more so than Saba. She was the one who was just about to give birth to Maya when we first heard about my diagnosis and she is the one who had had to keep everything together during almost a year of treatment. This was a lovely moment.

We met when we were a fair bit younger and there is always a bit of debate about who it was that went for who! Saba was working in Selfridges in Birmingham and we just started chatting. I am sure I was trying to play it cool for a while but did eventually ask her out and things blossomed from there. Neither of us were giving much away at the start and I'm not one really a believer in love at first sight but Saba thinks there was something there from that first meeting. She was the first girl I had met where I actually felt really comfortable in her company. She was fun and bubbly but very homely, too. So, while we had great times going out, as young couples do, we were equally happy just chilling together on the sofa with a cup of tea.

I also knew that deep down she was a good human being. Dating is fun when you are young but, deep down, you can always be a little unsure about a partner's character. I knew Saba was family-orientated, quite like me, and it wasn't long before we were living together. At the age of 23 or 24, we were ready to settle down. Then Mila came along and it was a bit tricky as Saba was studying at university and I was travelling around with all my loan spells, living in different areas and in and out of hotels.

I think we are very similar in some ways, as well as having our differences, but we know each other inside out now. like most couples. I am not the easiest person to be around sometimes and certainly wasn't when I was playing football, but Saba is the one who knows how to deal with me and when to leave me alone. There are a lot of highs and lows in the game and you have to make sure you don't get too carried away with the good times or too despondent in the bad. In a sense, a career can swing from being on top of the world on a Saturday night to being in a really bad place by the Tuesday. Sometimes I may need to let off a bit of steam verbally, sometimes I might be very quiet, and Saba is not a passive character and can be feisty, but she was always great with how she understood all of the pressures.

There are a lot of other things associated with being a footballer as well, such as the nights out and the attention you receive, and that can be difficult for a partner. We have a really good understanding of each other and, as a rule of thumb, are generally both very laid-back, which is probably why we get on so well. We argue like most couples do but not really over anything silly and we are both very relaxed in each other's company. In fact, there was one argument we had during my treatment about whether we should take Mila out of school or not, and my mum looked on it as a positive as I was still voicing my opinion and we were having a lively discussion.

The way Saba dealt with everything that happened was incredible really. I am not sure many people will fully realise or understand what she had to contend with. I went through what I was going through but she had some very tough times as well, although with a different experience to me. She had just become a mother again, had two children to look after, including a baby, and I wasn't at home very much. And when I was, I couldn't do much to help. Having a new-born is difficult enough but, to do so with a partner who has just been diagnosed with cancer, well, that just adds to the challenge. Saba was having to deal with all of this while also holding it together for the sake of the kids and me.

Mila was in her first year of school and Maya had just been born, then there was the worry of seeing me ill, having to travel up and down to Manchester and everything else. Mothers are always so good at juggling things, aren't they? And Saba was having to juggle so much at that time. On a few occasions, I am sure there was only so much she could take. Even now, I still sometimes see the effects of everything she went through which have taken their toll. I think it has made her a lot more anxious, even if she maybe tries to hide it.

She has been through an ordeal – we all have – that makes us all understand that life isn't always a Disney fairytale. And it all came at a time when everything was wonderful and we were so happy and settled. She saw me go through everything and, now, she pays far more attention to anything that she sees about cancer on the television. Stories about people suffering from illnesses and going through tough times are something she notices far more. There is that concern and worry about all of her loved ones and our family, and our cupboards are now full of herbs and other remedies to suit every taste and illness. And I believe those effects of what happened will always be there. We will remember that time and have to deal with those memories.

We will get over it but we will never forget and, for Saba in particular, I think moving on has been difficult. What we certainly do is appreciate everything that we have now as a family. Maybe we took things for granted before. I think a lot of people do – you don't realise how much you take for granted until it looks like you might lose it all. We have never been what you might call a typical footballer and partner, the stereotype of a footballing couple who are a bit flashy and so on. We have always appreciated everything we had but that has been amplified massively now.

We are looking forward to the future while worrying about our kids' futures. Relationships are key to bringing up children and we are working together, as a team, to do the best we can for Mila and Maya. And since my illness, we spend more attention on deciding what we want to do with our lives and the time we want to spend together as a couple and a family. As one example, we really value our weekends now. That wasn't always possible when I was playing because there were my needs with having a game or training. That sounds very selfish, and maybe it is, but that's what football demands. After retiring, I promised to free up as much time as possible for my family, as well as me and Saba also needing time together. We are still young and still have moments we want to share together, which we try to do whenever we have the opportunity.

Nothing too crazy, just maybe finding somewhere quiet to talk, because it really is the simple things at times that are the nicest. We don't share the same interests all of the time but we do share a love for spirituality, self-learning and nature, and it all works really well for us together.

As well as Saba, there were obviously so many other people who were key to helping me through the treatment and getting me back home again, notably Mum, Dad and my sisters. Although my mum and dad have split up, they still get on really well and both helped me massively during the time I was in hospital. I always knew Mum was tough but I found out she was even tougher than I thought. That's mums for you. They just keep on going through everything.

It must have been difficult for her and, in truth, I can't begin to imagine how difficult. She was up to see me whenever I needed it, maybe for a couple of days during the week when Mila was at school so Saba stayed at home, as well as carrying on working and helping Saba when she could. At other times, she would call me and would be able to tell from my voice if I was struggling and would then be straight up the motorway to visit me. I was struggling to cook, to make healthy food, so she would come and do it for me. I had gone vegan, so I wasn't touching meat or fish, and Mum wasn't vegan, but she would still cook whatever I wanted. Then she would be tidying the apartment because I was too tired to move from my bed or the chair.

All the practical stuff that was needed, Mum was there, and this is without even going into the emotional side of her son being faced with a battle to survive. She has seen me in some really dark situations, as has Saba. They have seen me at my worst. For anyone to see their son go through what I went through can't have been nice, particularly as I seemed to pick up every complication going during the treatment. But she would never complain and, once she got over the initial shock of the diagnosis, she said she always felt I would come through it.

She was always protective, too. There were times when I was struggling and Mum would have to carry the shopping and other items. She actually said to me at one point that the one good thing about my illness is that we got to spend some time together. Football is so selfish as a sport and you don't realise it when you are right in the thick of it. But I didn't see my mum enough and I remember once asking her what she wanted for her birthday, and she replied: "Just a bit of your time, Carl." I can see it all now, the same with Saba, because I was always such an obsessive when it came to football that I didn't see enough of Mum and Dad. Everyone takes a back seat when you are playing football.

So, as crazy as it sounds in such a horrible scenario, while I was ill and having treatment, I got to spend more time with my parents. Dad is a fairly quiet character now, he doesn't say much. He probably found what happened to me harder to deal with. He never gave much away and I remember looking at him a few times and could see him thinking about everything and I just didn't know how he was doing or coping with it. The one time I was back home and he was going to drive me up to Christie's, he just sat there in the car on the drive and broke down. I don't know if he had cried before or been holding it in but I think he could see how bad I was and it was getting to him. He would see me struggling to even pick my bag up and found it difficult to see what I had become.

My Dad is a tough man too, always has been. He came over from Nigeria to study IT at Aston University and to look after my grandad when he had sickle cell. He managed a qualification in computer programming and was in and out of different jobs. I remember him working in Banbury for a bit and would do well in something, make some decent money and then not work for a bit. I remember we would know when things were going well because we would get a few extra treats. But it rarely lasted!

As I grew older, he'd be looking after places, security-style, and he'd be around the community making sure there wasn't any trouble. He was a strong man, well respected and well liked around the area. As a teenager, I'd be with Dad on a Friday night in the Spitfire, which was a rough pub, then he'd have to go off to the curry house at 11pm to check it was alright, as well as the local Spar.

That was ironic really, as my mates used to hang around outside that shop. If they were getting up to any mischief, they would soon stop if Dad arrived. I remember going to school one day and hearing that he had given one of them a whack. One of my mates had got a bit chirpy, so Dad smacked him. Strangely enough, I don't think my mate was quite as chirpy again for a while.

Just like my mum, the silver lining to me having blood cancer was being able to spend a lot of time with my dad, which was good. We'd sit and watch TV together and I'd be chatting to him, talking about Nigeria and what was going on there. We could sit there for hours talking about the traditions of the country and discussing when we could go back. This time together was really special, because while Dad was always in my life, asking around for lifts all the time to get me to training and spending weekends together when I was a teenager, we are just so much closer now.

It was nice for the two of us to have that quality time together and, when something like this happens, it very quickly makes you realise that nothing lasts forever. When you think that you might not be around for ever, you know that other people might not be around for ever either. And it is so important to have no regrets about whether you spent enough time together. I always see Mum and Dad regularly now, or make sure we are in contact with a call or text message every few days at the least. It's the same with my sisters, who I'd probably not seen as much of before.

They were at college and university – Tayla, who is Mum's daughter, and Tia, who is Dad's. Tia handled it really well on a quiet level. She is a really tough young woman. She would be saying: "He's my brother, he's tough. Don't worry, because he's going to be alright." There was some belief there, that's for sure.

Tayla would come up and visit with Mum and was at an age where she was still dependent on her as well. She probably had to grow up quickly with everything that happened to me.

My friends, Adam, Robbie and Sylvan, were the ones who would often come and visit me and be ready when needed. When they arrived, we could just sit around and act normally, and spend a day in the apartment in Manchester. When I needed certain foods or just fancied something home-cooked, they would ferry it up from Birmingham and bring other health foods. Anything to help me in getting better. They might come up and watch the football, or just for a quick chat. Then, if I was well enough to get out, we might head somewhere close for a bite to eat, which would be a nice breather. I just needed some normality from what I was going through at times and I think they had seen that.

Of course they would ask how I was but then we would be just as we are for most of the time, relaxed together and joking about. Seeing them would give me a boost and it would give me the energy to get out of bed, which was good. I had so much support from a lot of people but they really were there for me and are the definition of friends that have become family. Like a lot of people, they wanted to do anything they could do to help and there wasn't a week that went by where they didn't want to try and come up to see me.

So, between family and friends, there was always someone around when needed and I will always be grateful for that. Everyone would try and do their little bit when they could and I know it was a huge relief to everybody when I was in remission and back home. I never wanted any fuss, or to put people out, but, for so many of my family, life had almost come to a stop after I was diagnosed. Their lives were all on hold. No-one could really make any plans too far ahead in the future.

Tayla turned 18 in the December midway through my treatment but we couldn't celebrate it properly so we had that a year later – when she was 19! Life had to revolve around me to a certain extent, although I didn't want it to. But, with the news that I was on the mend, everyone was able to get on with things and hopefully get back to a normal life, which was all we really wanted.

23

Hanging up the gloves

So many people had supported me during my treatment and, once I had settled back into life at home, one big announcement remained; to tell the world that I had played my last game of football, both for Wolves and for Nigeria. Before that of course came the World Cup in Russia, for which I had played that very first qualifier for Nigeria in Zambia. It felt strange watching the tournament finals, particularly as I knew I was going to be retiring. I knew that I would never again be turning out for the Super Eagles, which had given me so much pleasure over the last couple of years of my career.

I just had a feeling early in the treatment that it could be the end of my football. It obviously wasn't the priority – the first thought was staying alive and getting better – but I just had that feeling my career was over, even without knowing the ordeal I was about to go through. If I had been aware at that stage of the effects the treatment would have on my body, I would have known for sure that I would soon be hanging up my gloves.

I just knew in those early weeks and months that it was going to be very tough to play again and I was wrestling with the prospect that my time could be done. It wasn't something I was constantly thinking about but, when I had a bit of time to myself, I conceded that I didn't think I would be able to play again. It was towards the end of the treatment journey that I started speaking to my doctor, Adrian, and he just confirmed what I was thinking. He told me that my organs had seen so many toxins going through them that it might be dangerous to play on.

I won't deny that it was a sad moment, as it is for anyone when they decide to call it a day, whether that's in football or any other career for that matter. But, equally, given everything I had been through, I was happy to accept it from

Adrian and it wasn't something I was going to question or argue with. My priorities had changed. The mixed feelings stemmed a lot from all the time and effort that had been put into me in the game, the people who had pushed me along the way and helped me to become a footballer in the first place.

Times were never easy for Mum and Dad when I was growing up, yet they never gave up on me and did everything they could to help me with my football. I think back now on the times they managed to get me to different places when we didn't have a car. Scraping money together for buses or taxis to get me to training, arranging lifts for me with other people, still getting me into Wolves once a week when we couldn't really afford it any more.....all of that helped get me where I was and to have a successful career. That was what I felt most sad about now it was coming to an end.

I know my mum was worried about what I would do once I had to hang up my boots but I felt quite comfortable about the situation. I had hardly spoken to Wolves about football matters during my treatment and certainly not about retirement. They just asked me how I was doing, whether I needed anything and I knew they were there if I ever needed them. The matter of whether I was going to carry on playing was never a priority in anyone's mind really. Was I going to retire? The bigger question was whether I was going to be alive. That was the most crucial point.

I had another conversation with Adrian once I was back home and told him I was definitely going to stop. I didn't want to send Wolves managing director Laurie Dalrymple or the sporting director Kevin Thelwell a text. It felt like something I needed to tell them face-to-face, so we met up for a bite to eat at a pub in Harborne. Wolves' chairman Jeff Shi, part of the owners Fosun, came along as well, so the three of them heard together in our chat that I was going to retire. It was all very much: 'Thanks for everything you have done but I'm not going to be able to play any more'. I told them it wasn't about feeling sad or having any regrets because there was a bigger battle I needed to win. I was just happy to be there and happy to be able to have the conversation with them.

I have to say that I felt nervous about seeing them, probably because I knew that once I had told them, the wheels would be set in motion and there would be no going back. I was wrestling in my mind how the conversation was going to go and how I was going to word it. I'd had a week or so between talking to the doctor and going to see them and found it difficult to get the words out. They made it easy for me, though, and said they and the club would support me with anything I needed to do. I went into Wolves a few days later to meet the players, staff and everyone behind the scenes to say an official goodbye and do an interview and photograph for the official announcement which would follow.

There were still a lot of staff there who I had known for a very long time. Doc Perry, for example, who had to phone me with the news all those months previously that I had contracted leukaemia. I had known the Doc for about 15 years and had been speaking to him throughout my treatment. He was another person in the medical profession I could speak to because even if he wasn't a specialist in haematology, I could ask him about so much other stuff. He was getting to see all the correspondence outlining how the treatment was going and it was nice to listen to someone else's opinion.

Doc Perry, Matt, is still my doctor now. If I had a problem, he would always be someone I would trust. I would literally trust him with my life and I know he will always take my call. The same goes for Phil Hayward, Wolves' head of medical, who was massively helpful for me and would also come up and see me to make sure he kept in touch. I knew I had so much support from colleagues at Wolves, both people who were still there and others who had moved on. I had loads of messages off the goalkeeping coaches I had worked for like Pat Mountain and Bobby Mimms, and visits from so many of my team-mates including Sylvan Ebanks-Blake, Leon Clarke, Ethan Ebanks-Landell, Danny Batth and Dave Edwards. And obviously Matt Murray was someone I am very close to and he was the one I confided in when the treatment was at its worst and I lost my sight with the sepsis. Matt came to see me with Joe Hart early on, which was also a big boost, and so many people from the world of football got in touch.

Going back to confirm my retirement was strange as it was the first time I had been back to the club since leaving for one of those tests that previous summer. That seemed like an age ago and driving through the gates after so long felt a bit weird. Also, near the end of my treatment, on one of the days I came back on the train, it passed through Wolverhampton. For a moment, just for a moment, I thought about getting off and walking up the road to look at the stadium again. I decided against in the end, so it was nice to get back to Compton soon afterwards. I still felt at home there, although I was not long out of treatment and feeling really weak.

I had changed a lot during the year and the training ground had, too – it took a bit of time to get my bearings. I was looking around the pitches wondering how on earth I used to get about them playing in goal. Even if there was some sadness during the visit, I knew it wasn't a forever thing. The football decision was final but I knew I'd still be welcome to pop into the club and do different things. So it was a hello and a goodbye, and see you around soon!

Then Wolves announced the news, complete with a video from so many of the world's top goalkeepers showing their support. That was just incredible. I didn't know it was coming and it was my friend who saw it first and tipped me off. I thought the announcement would go out, a statement and interview, and all would be done and dusted. So that was a really nice surprise. Seeing some of my idols on that video wishing me all the best, I was a bit starstruck. Peter Schmeichel, Gianluigi Buffon, so many more, I didn't think these people even knew my name, let alone have time to send me a message of support. It was mad! The whole thing was emotional and the support I was receiving from fans, from everyone, was amazing.

Obviously, it was a time of reflection having decided that the football was now over, as the game had played such a huge part of my life. And when I stopped to think about the career I had enjoyed, I felt so fortunate and privileged. If someone had said to me, or more to the point my goalkeeping coach, when I was 16 or 17, that I would go on and enjoy the career I did, I would have snapped their hand off. To play as many games as I did for Wolves makes me extremely proud. I played with so many top players and competed against some top goalkeepers who became great friends. To be part of that history of keepers at Wolves, where there have been some absolutely fantastic players, was an incredible feeling. Even in League One, which no-one wanted to be in, to be involved in that clean sheet record, which will forever be connected with that team, is very special.

I had some great times as well in my loan spells at clubs like QPR, Leicester and Middlesbrough, and at a young age it was such a good experience to go and take on a challenge somewhere else, which is what I would always say to young players today. Then to go on and make over 200 appearances for Wolves, it is nice to think I will hopefully always be remembered for my football achievements and be remembered around Wolverhampton. You don't tend to get too many players nowadays who have one club which they can always be associated with and be held in such fond regard. And my relationship with Wolves and the fans is probably a lot closer than most, because of the illness and the support I received.

I know a lot people outside Wolverhampton probably look at me as someone who has had leukaemia, but I would also imagine that when they think of me in football terms, they will connect me to Wolves rather than anywhere else. I had the Wolves connection with football long before the illness and I am very proud to call myself 'a Wolves man'. The fans always had my back as well, even in the football, long before I was diagnosed. When I walked out to play at Molineux or on the road, and had those fans in the stands behind me, I knew they would always give me support. Sometimes, fans become frustrated at players and I am sure the Wolves fans had their frustrations with me, but they were always willing to forgive and always willing me to do well. If I made a mistake, it was never really abuse, more a case of 'Come on Carl, better luck next time'.

When I was dropped for that spell in the Championship, the fans weren't happy. I remember going on against Burnley in the second half when Emi Martinez was injured, and the reception was unbelievable. The whole stadium was singing my name and that doesn't normally happen for a goalkeeper introduced from the bench. Normally, I am right in the zone when I am playing, totally and utterly focused, but I have to say that moment knocked me out of my stride – it was a mad situation.

So I always had that great connection with the fans and it was wonderful to be able to get back to Molineux and go on the pitch before the second home game of the 2018/19 season, against Manchester City. I didn't want a big deal made about it or a huge build-up, so they just mentioned it a few minutes before kick-off and out I went. I was still in a phase of not wanting to be around too many people and that was my big worry. It was nice, though, to go out and wave to the fans as a sign of my thanks and appreciation for the support I had received. Wolves fans had been so good to me, not just through my treatment but throughout my career. Goalkeeper can be a lonely position but I always felt the fans had my back in every game I played. I was with Mila and my Godson and it was very emotional. I could feel the love out there that everyone had given me.

I hadn't been inside Molineux for a while and felt so small on the pitch, standing there and looking around the packed stadium. It was good to catch up with people behind the scenes and see the fans again, the first time people had seen me for a long time, and another moment I will always remember as very special. Despite being quite paranoid about being around people and running the risk of picking up germs, it was another great experience, although I got out of there very quickly afterwards. Mila and my Godson were really giggly on the pitch but I think they enjoyed it, too! Mila isn't really interested in football but was buzzing to be on the pitch and was loving the attention. It was crazy that she was there again having been to the first game of the previous season against Middlesbrough when everyone had shown their support. She had no idea why she was out on the pitch with me but, at some point, she will find out. Like any dad, I think you hope that you can make your children proud and even if she isn't interested in football, it will be nice to sit down and look at the footage one day when she is older and have those memories of being out there together.

Memories ended up being all I had left of my football but I still felt very comfortable with the decision. Of course I'd have liked to have played more games, won more trophies, any player would, but I had enjoyed my career and had to accept why and how it had ended. If there was one thing that maybe rankled a little bit, it was on missing out on the World Cup with Nigeria.

I don't feel any ill-will against what happened to me with my illness. After those early 'why me?' thoughts, I just got my head down and got on with it. Acceptance – that was what it was. I accepted what had happened and set about overcoming it. But the one thing, the only thing, I feel was taken away from me in my career was the opportunity to play in a World Cup finals. That chance, that opportunity…..it's something you dream of as a kid, the pinnacle of representing your country on the biggest stage of all.

I believed we would qualify, as we did, and I believe I would have kept my place and played in the World Cup. I don't think that feeling will ever leave me but I just have to deal with it. No matter what you achieve in your career, or the money that you earn, it isn't about that. It is about the achievements and the experiences, and being involved in tournaments like the World Cup. I would never want to change or replace anything that happened in my football career but missing out on that experience is the one thing I feel was taken away and that is what I will always have a sense of sadness about. Even more so as Nigeria had a warm-up game against England at Wembley when I would most likely have played as well.

I was close to going to the game as I was invited to attend but I had only just finished my treatment and it was too much of a risk too soon. To actually play against England at Wembley would have been another dream come true as well – and not the place outside Mum and Dad's flat that we used to call Wembley! It was that game and watching the World Cup on television that made it all hit home and did make me emotional to think what I was missing out on. That feeling of knowing I would never get an opportunity like that again and just realising I was never going to be playing football again.

I had so much support from Nigeria, just like Wolves, and that made a really positive difference. The players, the coaching staff and the Nigerian FA all supported me through everything and were always there for me and still are. Although I have retired, I still speak to a lot of them today. To have grown up dreaming of playing for Nigeria and then achieved it at an age when I was probably old enough to really appreciate it, is something I will cherish for the rest of my life.

Putting it all together, I played around 200 games for Wolves, earning two promotions and briefly appearing in the Premier League. I also represented Nigeria, a country with over 200 million people around the world. Just thinking about it now still gives me goosebumps. So, yes, as I decided to retire and looked back on my career, it's fair to say I was reflecting on how far I had come from messing around outside our flat and starting out in Chelmsley Wood.

While I always loved football and was very grateful for the career I had, I don't think I properly enjoyed it until I was 25 or 26. Until then, I always had a fear about games and worried about the week of training and what might go wrong. It might sound strange but when I got to my mid to late 20s, I realised I could actually enjoy it all a bit more. I know fans might not understand it and it seems strange saying it because being a footballer is such a great profession. But I am just talking about the pressure and how with all the games it is then difficult to enjoy your down time. It is only after I retired that I fully understood how I felt that pressure and expectation every single day. I wouldn't say it was a bad pressure or a burden or something I couldn't handle, but it was always there. I was always putting that pressure on myself, the pressure to perform every day and getting in that mindset of giving it my all.

Every day, I was watching what I was eating and then looking at the other keepers and wondering what they were eating and what they were doing in the gym. What were they doing to try and be better than me and take my place? I remember telling Saba about it and it was only after I finished that I realised just how obsessed I was with it all. Obsessed with what I was going to do before training, thinking about it as soon as I got up in the morning, on the way in. Thinking about what I was going to do before I started the warm-up. It got to the point where I was worried about what warm-up I needed to do before the team did a warm-up before going outside to do another warm-up.

Then, after training, what could I do in the gym to make myself better? What should I do to recover properly? What should I eat for lunch? And then later in the week, I would start to worry about the game on the Saturday. It was a battle in my mind, going over all the different possibilities and eventualities of what might go wrong. That kept me on edge, in a good way, that pressure, and then the relief if you won and could breathe again for a while. Until the next training session, or game, of course.

Later in my career, I still felt those emotions but was able to relax a little and enjoy everything a bit more as a result. And that's the thing – if I didn't feel that pressure or was too relaxed, I didn't like it either. I suppose that is what I miss to a certain extent and something I have had to come to terms with – that buzz and that pressure, which I enjoyed, but made me something of an obsessive.

Playing football has been such a massive positive in my career and life and the only regret I have is that I didn't play more. But it is definitely a selfish career. When I think back to all the feelings I had, getting two buses and a train when I was at the academy, all the hours I put in and that people put in with me. All the support I had from Mum and Dad. Everything revolved around me and my football. I wasn't being selfish for selfish's sake but because I had to be selfish to get to where I wanted to be.

Everything I had achieved, the football journey I had been on, it had spanned over 20 years and now it was over. Uttering the words 'I am retiring', followed by the official announcement, made it final. In the grand scheme of things, compared to what I had been through, football was great but now I wanted to carry on and make sure I was here for my family. Football was fantastic for me and it was my passion but it was not my priority now.

At times, I had got lost in life, we all do, and football had perhaps taken over to the extent that I didn't spend enough time with my family. And, having come out of football, I now realise that the game doesn't define me. Although I love football and loved playing, I am no less of a person because I can't play anymore. It gave me some of the best times of my life but everything must come to an end and my career would have finished eventually, even if the plan was for retirement to have come many years later.

But it had happened – what will be will be – and even without football, I am still a father, a son, a brother, a husband. So now, yes, with the football finished, it was on to the next chapter. It was all about my family and my future.

24

Everything to live for

My family and my future. It sounds straightforward but we all know life isn't that simple. I felt like a cancer patient for at least six months after coming home. I still do to a degree even now, writing this. But being diagnosed and treated changed a lot of my outlook on life. It forced me to go deeper emotionally as I couldn't just rely on my body. I had to go inside myself. So, although my body was in a catastrophic mess at times, my mind and spirit were seeing life crystal-clear. We can spend a lifetime chasing money, cars or whatever material items we crave but ultimately it is love, laughter and experiences with people that prove to be the most precious. And they can't be bought.

I had never loved so much in my life as I did during those 12 months in hospital. The time I spent with family and friends was really special to me and, although it was the toughest test in my life, it was also the best time of my life. I had the chance to experience a hug or a kiss from my children like it was my last, a conversation with Saba like it was my last, reminiscing with my Mom and Dad like it was my last and some laughter with my friends as if it was my last. I had a chance to receive and show love in a way I never had before and I can truly thank cancer for that.

About six months after I arrived home, I was watching a TV show with one of my favourite spiritual healers, Ram Dass, who said: "I don't wish you a stroke but I wish you the grace from a stroke." In just one line, he had explained what I had been feeling for the previous 18 months. I would not wish for anyone to go through the pain and trauma I went through but, if only I could pass my appreciation for life through someone else's body! I feel truly alive and there was a time in hospital when I was finally able to go outside, that just to have a deep breath of fresh air felt like such a blessing.

Of course, there are still many obstacles in life. I have had fears, and still do from time to time. When I came out of hospital, I had fears of being in crowded places, fears of suffering a relapse and fears of slipping back into forgetting what my real values are. I felt my fears were something I had to sit down and really assess, because trying to run away from them is a race that never, ever finishes. Many people worry about things they can't control or things that are never going to happen – we all have that voice in our head that nags at us. Sometimes we can have a fight in our heads about a scenario or event that hasn't happened and is never going to come along, and becoming aware of this fight is the first stage of dealing with it. As I sit down to contemplate why something scares me, I can find reasons why it does and put some perspective into my thoughts. I can find that this fear or these thoughts aren't healthy for me, so then I can try to find peace with it.

Gradually, I started to get back on my feet after my intensive treatment. My body had been through a lot in the space of a year, my hair and body were thin, but I got round to restarting on all the normal things like watching my children in school plays, going for walks, getting back in the gym and having the family around to visit. My weight started to come back while my energy levels increased, so I spent more time doing things that make me happy like going to the gym, boxing and cycling. There are still times when I have to take a break but it's about finding a balance in something I enjoy doing.

In the back of my mind, there is always a part of me which thinks I can still play football, but I've come to know I really can't. That's the reality and I have happily accepted it. Whatever I decide to do from here will be based around my happiness – that is what will drive me. I still love football dearly, don't get me wrong, and I always will. But I needed that break from it because I'd been involved in it and playing pretty constantly from the age of six or seven. Wolves and football had been my addiction for decades and my mind, body and soul had gone into it, so I have had to peel that back a bit and just be a fan now.

The club have been great with me with everything, whether it's the media work or just inviting me back to watch training and speak to the coaches. And when I go in, I have to confess that I do get that bit of a buzz back. Watching Nigeria play reminds me of the joy that playing international football brought but, of course, missing the World Cup still niggles at me from time to time and is one of the voices in my head. So maybe, just maybe, I have unfinished business there in terms of the national set-up.

I see football as a bit like a marriage. You can't really be in one of those part-time, can you? You have to give it your all when you are married and it's the same with football. I feel that if ever I feel like I want to go back into football, I have to be totally ready and fully committed and, yes, be back married to the game. Maybe we are just having a bit of a cooling-off period at present and a bit of a break– we shall see! It is more important that I am trying to do things which make me happy and are good for my family. Part of this thinking is about leaving a legacy for my children.

Time is not guaranteed, I know that now, so I am focused on trying to be a good role model to my kids. Writing this book is a part of that and something I thought long and hard about in hospital. Growing up, I never thought I'd be someone that might one day be thinking of doing a book like this, but with everything I have been through, if it just helps a few people who are going through the same thing, then hopefully it has been worth it. There was also that motivation about making my kids proud and trying to show them a good example in life. I cycled 100 miles for charity by taking part in the Velo Birmingham event in May of this year, so helping others is something else I really want to do. And I have plans in place for an even bigger charity bike ride in 2020, going via all the clubs I have played for. There were certainly a few!

It has been a year or so of getting back to spending more time with family and friends, seeing people more where previously I never had the time, and enjoying the simple things as I head into a new phase of my life. I am still having treatment for my leukaemia, it is still part of me, and will be for another year or more yet. In this book, I know I have been very honest and at times graphic about what I went through. And for people who may have been diagnosed with the disease, or any sort of cancer, that might have been difficult to read.

But what I would also say, just like so many stories I heard while I was receiving treatment, is that I have come out on the other side.

I am often asked what I would say to people who have been similarly diagnosed, which I guess is a question a lot of patients are asked. It's a very difficult one, because every person is different and every situation is different. And when you first get that diagnosis, and first hear those words, it is frightening.

It's never as simple as just saying to someone to 'be strong' and 'keep fighting'. While you always appreciate that sort of support, it is about so much more. In my case, I knew my biggest strength throughout the process was going to be my mind. That was exactly the same as in football where I had the physical attributes – but my mind was always the strongest. Having that positive mind-frame during the treatment was so important and if you can try to steer towards a positive outcome – or if that's not possible then a different outlook on life – I feel it helps massively. It is what helps you through the toughest times when you are feeling at rock bottom.

Acceptance was something that was so important for me. Accepting what was going on and getting on with trying to recover. When you are fighting with thoughts of 'why me?' and 'it's not fair, I don't deserve this', it doesn't help. I had a battle for a day or two with that and it didn't help me, so then it was about moving on and changing focus. 'Why Not Me?' as the title of this book says. Why shouldn't I be one of those people to be diagnosed with cancer?

I don't mean acceptance in the sense of meekly accepting what is going to happen, but accepting what you are going through.

Countless patients had come through it and had come out positively on the other side. And you have to remember that cancer can hit anyone, in any walk of life, at any time. Meeting that taxi driver whose son had the same cancer as me made me feel lucky in a way, because that could have happened to my kids. I would much rather me be the one who was fighting it, not them. Everyone would have thought my life was perfect before my diagnosis and it probably was. But that doesn't matter when cancer comes along.

There were of course times when thoughts of 'what if I don't make it?' flashed through my head. But I told Saba that no matter what happened, if things didn't work out and the worst came to the worst, it wouldn't be because I had quit. It would just mean that the disease had got the better of me and my body hadn't been able to fight it. I know that, very sadly, some don't make it and come through, and I can't even begin to explain or imagine what that must be like.

This disease has affected so many lives, so I don't want to come out like no hero. But if I have managed in this book to explain or offer an insight into what goes on, it might give people some understanding next time they see a friend or family member dealing with cancer.

Acceptance was key for me because, when I came to terms with my situation, it was a far happier place for me to be. I started to plan for what I was going to do afterwards and the things I would want to arrange when I was better. Even when I couldn't guarantee that I was going to make it, I was planning summer holidays with the kids, being able to get to my friend Adam's wedding and various other activities I could only take on after I had finished the treatment. It was all in my mind in planning my future. I had positive visions in my head and needed to have that to look forward to, as you do have so much time to think.

I would meditate in the morning when I could and have visions of laughing with my kids. Life is beautiful – I knew that before and I know it even more now. We all have tough times, everyone, but life is so worth fighting for and I had everything to live for. That is why I was never going to give up, no matter how bad the situation became. Not a chance.

It is probably difficult to think about if you haven't had that experience. Whether it's cancer, mental health issues, being abused, there are so many truly horrible things that people have to experience, but imagine the appetite for life you have if you can somehow get yourself through it. So please don't wait for a bad experience in life to start really living, experiencing and appreciating what you do have.

I hope this story can help people and myself to rethink all the situations we moan about that really haven't got any substance, when compared with the fact there are people on this earth fighting for their lives every minute. This gratitude is something I will never let myself forget and has put me in a place that I really want to be. When you are diagnosed with a life-threatening condition and there is a chance your time may come to an end, what do you value most? People and experiences. Those kisses and hugs off Mila and Maya just feel so much sweeter now.

I feel fortunate to have enjoyed the career I had in football, to have done something for a living which I always dreamed of and worked with fantastic people and enjoyed some successes. I feel just as fortunate now to have this new lease of life and renewed positivity, spending more time with the people I love and looking at different options for my next chapter. So much has happened to me since I sat crying in the car outside Homebase after receiving the worst possible news – the news which tore my world apart at a time when my life was at its wonderful best.

So many battles, so much pain, so much upheaval, but I feel better, stronger and closer to my family and friends than I ever did before that diagnosis and what followed it. And, after all that, when I think back to that day when my world was suddenly rocked in such a dramatic and drastic direction, do you know what?

I never did buy that paint.

Final thoughts

By Paul Berry

"Are you on your own?" The start of a phone conversation with then Wolves' managing director Laurie Dalrymple, in early July of 2017. Rarely a good sign. Laurie had an excellent way of breaking bad or difficult news which needed quick communication. And, at a busy football club, where no two days are the same, crisis management was a key part of the role of head of media. "Are you on your own?" No, I wasn't, sat in what at the time was a makeshift press office on the second floor of the Sir Jack Hayward building of the training ground. I headed outside and walked. All was quiet. We were in early July, the schools had broken up. It was a lovely sunny day – but not for long.

"I'm sorry to say I've got some really bad news," said Laurie. "It's Carl... he's been diagnosed with leukaemia." Silence. Stunned silence. That's not the sort of call you can be even slightly prepared for. My mind raced back a few days. I had been in reception at Compton and heard Carl chatting openly about needing to go for a check-up as he'd been suffering nose bleeds. He is a strong person is Carl, one of the strongest you could meet. So, it was the way he said 'I'm sure it's nothing' that reflected some concern in his voice. But leukaemia? Not leukaemia. Not to such a powerful, strapping footballer in his prime. But cancer, as so many people so cruelly experience, is indiscriminate.

The conversation moved on to what might happen, how the news would filter out, how the club could respond, how best to support Carl. Those situations, where there's real personal involvement for someone at the club, are so different to anything else you are faced with in a football press office. Yes, you still have to organise the press statements, the communications to relevant people before news is released, speak to the media, handle questions. But this isn't just a football situation. It's not about losing a game. With apologies to the legend of Bill Shankly, this is real life. This is the important stuff.

Things moved fast, with the statement agreed with the club's medical staff and Carl, and the players informed after being assembled by Nuno Espirito Santo in the training ground dressing room. There were a few tears as those players discovered the news a few minutes before it was officially made public. Even that was tough to see. Footballers are hardened to all manner of challenges which they front up on a daily basis. This one knocked them completely off their feet.

Then, with incredible speed and solidarity, the Wolves fans got to work. Some statements and stories are met with a huge response at the very point of pressing that 'send' button. This was undoubtedly one. The football world rallied round and messages streamed in not only from the Wolves fraternity but from local rivals, nationally and even across the globe. Good-luck wishes came from the likes of David De Gea and Barcelona keeper Marc-Andre ter Stegen. Later in the year, Brazilian legend Kaka posed with a 'Get Well Kemes' t-shirt.

As Carl braced himself for his toughest journey, the football family mobilised rapidly and, amid such devastating news, there was a strong will – even a need – to do something positive, to get behind the Wolves keeper and help others in a similar position. The indefatigable Steve Plant was soon in touch and Wolfie's Den was booked for a 24-hour penalty shootout and WV1 for a family day as the club and fans worked with Cure Leukaemia to show support.

The first team, under-23 and under-18 squads had photos taken with a banner backing Carl, as well as all the other office departments from Molineux and Compton. 'Team Kemes' was developing into a powerful force, just when the man himself needed it most. Because cancer of any type is indiscriminate, there is no reason why it should be more surprising when it afflicts a pro footballer built on power and athleticism. Yet it still seemed so unfair and ill-timed on Carl. For him, life at Wolves had blossomed and, after so many loan spells, he had made the position his and became a major influence in the dressing room.

Carl is friendly and fantastic company, one you can rely on in so many areas and who always represented Wolves with class and distinction. He was once part of a group of players who visited the Good Shepherd Centre's Soup Kitchen in the city centre, to serve lunch to some of the most vulnerable members of society. For an hour and a half, he mucked in, made sure every single person received their meal and openly chatted to all who wanted to. A week later, I received a call, saying he was in the city centre with a car full of items to donate to the Good Shepherd...and where should he report to donate them? That is Carl. Generous, knowledgable and thinking. He took that attitude into his media interviews, always ensuring he was enthusiastic and courteous.

It is that caring, open personality that inspired many thousands to support his recovery. It showed on the national stage when the FA kindly allowed Telford Wolves to fly the flag of support for him at a pre-World Cup Wembley friendly.

Come the end of 2017/18, there was more positive news. The pinging of his tweet confirming his remission was undoubtedly the best social media item all summer. "Are you on your own?" Thankfully, Carl wasn't. Everyone had his back. And, amid many more challenges ahead, they will continue to do so.

So where did the book idea come from? Not long before Christmas, mid-way through his treatment, Carl again appeared on the phone. He had read that a book I had been working on with his former Wolves team-mate Dave Edwards had just been published. "I kept seeing you pair disappear at the training ground and wondered what you were up to," he chuckled. A pause, then: "Don't put your pen away. I might have something to say in a few months."

Carl made notes about his experiences when up to it and then, over many hours, we talked it all through, with no stone left unturned. From a happy but far from luxurious upbringing, to the ups and downs of a rollercoaster career which ended at its peak as first choice with Wolves and Nigeria, to the challenge literally to stay alive through such a gruelling challenge…this is Carl's story. From the Village Hotel at Walsall to Wolverhampton Lawn Tennis and Squash Club. From the Green House pub in Sutton to Cineworld on Birmingham's Broad Street. Much conversation, bucketloads of tea, coffee and water and a fascinating and sometimes harrowing insight into the incredible journey. 'Why Not Me?', a title Carl chose, is testament to his selflessness and mental strength. It tells how he accepted cancer into his life without rancour or bitterness and vowed not to let it hang around too long; and how his mind would never, ever let him down.

There are many people to thank – Carl's partner Saba, who checked the text and added her own contribution; his mum Jackie, who bravely re-read a diary compiled during his treatment and provided fond memories and pictures; David Instone, a long-standing purveyor of wise counsel and encouragement, and his wife Liz, who have designed the pages and overseen the organisation process; to Carl's friend Michelle Maycock for the excellent cover imagery, front and back; Simon Pagett from Synaxis Design for making said cover look fantastic; and official Wolves photographer Sam Bagnall for his chronicling of Carl's career on the inside pages. Also to Matt Murray for his recollections and publicity help.

From me, a big thank-you to Carl. I feel lucky to have worked with fantastic people at Wolves in my media office years and feel privileged to have followed my role in Dave's autobiography by now assisting Carl. To have been trusted by him to help tell his story – from which I have learned much – has been fascinating and hugely appreciated. Hopefully, we have done it justice.

Final thoughts

By Carl's mum Jackie

Carl was as good as gold growing up. Like a lot of lads, as long as he was playing football, he was happy, and didn't need to be wandering the streets with his friends and so on. His Dad, Ike, was a very good tennis player but had Carl kicking a ball from a very young age, probably from the moment he could walk.

There was a real community feel around our flat and, as soon as the kids got older, they would play outside, using my washing line as the goal. So most of the time, we always knew where they were. I never thought I was too strict with Carl but maybe I was from time to time! I do remember sticking a load of washing-up liquid in his mouth after he swore.

Football was another family for Carl and that kept him disciplined and gave him something to aim for, which maybe some of the other kids didn't have, so they went down a different path. I am sure I don't know everything that went on and am sure Carl wasn't golden in his behaviour all the time but he didn't give us many problems. He has always been laid-back and was late for school a few times but he did okay there without perhaps pushing himself too hard. He didn't necessarily do all of the homework he was set but he went to school and that was good enough.

Having seen how some others went at that time, I am quite proud that he behaved as he did. As parents, we can only do so much and what he achieved is very much down to him and his dedication. We were aware of what can go wrong with kids growing up and we didn't want Carl going down that route. It was good that he had the football to aim for, although it's fair to say I never thought he would become a professional. Ike was all about him getting a good education and we were just parenting him and hoping it would all turn out alright.

I know Carl has written about some of the things that went on with the racism we suffered as a white woman going out with a black man but, for the most part, we were able to get on with our lives. And there were plenty of good times we enjoyed as he was growing up. We never had much money and often had to buy presents on the 'never never' but we made sure Carl never went without. And he would always be happy enough with a football kit and a ball.

We certainly knew the value of everything and I didn't get on a plane until I was 40 and we went on holiday to France. We had a lot of caravan holidays, particularly in Devon, where my mum moved after losing my dad. My brother John was not much older than Carl and they would often go to Devon in the summer and have a great time. That was normal for us. We didn't know anyone who had a posh car and fancy holidays, so Carl didn't know anything different.

When it came to football, he played first for Castlehurst Colts, then Chelmsley Ravens and we would watch as much as we could. With Chelmsley, there would be training in the week and matches on a Sunday. I look back and remember one Sunday it really snowed, horrifically snowed, and he was stood in goal, freezing, with nothing to do. The lady who made the tea used to take us to games and on the way home, he was in the back crying as his hands were so cold. There was a good community in that team and we loved being part of it.

Then he was spotted by Aston Villa and started training at their academy. I remember a game at Manchester United, where we all went on the coach. It was rained off, so on the way home they stopped to give the lads breakfast. Carl was sat on his own while the others were huddled together and I felt a bit sorry for him. But he wasn't bothered, that was Carl. He was always comfortable around people he really knew and didn't feel the need to do anything to be accepted by anyone else. He probably only had a few friends as he was growing up but they were really good ones; people he was really happy to spend time with.

Eventually, he had enough at Villa. It was quite intense and he just said he didn't want to go back and preferred to go back and play with his Sunday League mates. When he tried again, at Wolves, it felt like a totally different set-up from the start. There wasn't as much pressure and they looked after the kids a bit better. Carl was also a bit older and could handle everything more easily. It was probably only then that we started to think he maybe had a chance of making it.

Sure enough, he did, first with the scholarship. I can remember all of us going along for the day, Carl doing his medical and then signing the forms to make it official. It was a great day for us all, but I was still wondering what might happen if he didn't make it. That's natural for a mum, I suppose!

It took him a long time to really crack it at Wolves, with all the loan spells and time on the substitutes' bench. But he worked so hard, even just managing to get himself to training when money was tight and he was in the academy.

Ike and I separated while he was a teenager but probably get on better now than we did before! We never moved far from each other and are always at family gatherings with our partners. I had a daughter Tayla and Ike had one, too, Tia. They are not called half-sisters. For Carl, they are his sisters. All of us get on really well and that was so important come the time he really needed us.

I won't ever forget the day of his diagnosis – Wednesday, July 5th, 2017. It was about 4 o'clock and I was at his nan's house. He phoned and said: "Are you alright, Mum?" I said 'yes' and he asked if I was at work. I said: "No, why? What do you want?" It was then that he let out this terrible cry and was sobbing, unable to get his words out. I don't know how long it went on for but it seemed like an eternity. I told Tayla we needed to get around to see him, with no idea of what we were going to find.

When we arrived, Saba, heavily pregnant, was in the window seat and Carl was on the settee. I can still recall the moment vividly, as Carl said he'd got blood cancer and feared he wasn't going to see his daughter grow up. Tayla screamed and I just sat down, dumbfounded. I didn't know what to think as we never had an inkling anything was wrong. We didn't even know he had been going for tests. I put my arm around him, said I was going to help him get through this and said we were going to do it right because we were only going to do it once. Then I had to get out and went to the bathroom.

After his Dad arrived, I walked the streets for a while, trying to take the news in and not wanting Carl to see how upset I was. I didn't say it at the time but of course that thought went through my head: 'Are we going to lose him?' I know a lot more about blood cancer now, we are all educated after this journey but I had absolutely no idea then. How could we say he was going to get well? We didn't know. I couldn't find the right words. The nightmare had begun.

I phoned the chip shop where I worked to say I needed the night off. The reality was: 'Would I ever be able to go back to work?' Hospital appointments at Heartlands became a daily event and that is where Stiliyan Petrov went to see Carl. We also met the consultant Manos for the first time. He handed a piece of paper to Carl, who passed it on to me. "Is this a guarantee that you are going to cure my son?" I asked. "Yes," he replied. That is a moment I will never forget.

We were on such an emotional rollercoaster and I have no idea how Carl felt but he was incredibly strong in those early days. There were major discussions about where to have treatment and the time at Heartlands brought back memories of when my dad was treated there for cancer many years before.

Carl decided on Christie's, which was like a breath of fresh air. It was a big room and it felt like it was where he needed to be, to go through his ordeal. We were still wondering how he was going to survive it and I thought, in those early weeks, that my crying might never stop. But it had to. I didn't want Carl to see how upset I was. That wasn't going to help him. As any parent would say, I'd rather take this myself than see a son or daughter go through it. He was young, fit, in his prime. So why him? And yet, as Carl himself said, why not him?

After the initial shock and speaking to the doctors, the feedback was very positive about what the treatment could achieve. So, once I got to grips with it, I truly believed he was going to be well again and that is where all my focus was going to be. The way he went into the treatment, and how strong he stayed, was an inspiration to all of us. I'm not sure I coped as well as he did.

Carl had his apartment and we wanted to make sure there was someone with him, especially when he was having his unwell periods. I remember the first time when it really got to me to see him struggling. I had spoken to Ike, who went on a Friday and said he wasn't well at all when he left. I told Tayla we needed to go as soon as I finished work on the Sunday. When we got there, he looked really ill. He said he wasn't eating anything, so I went to Sainsbury's for a cooked chicken. I watched him smelling the food and thought how poorly he looked. We left about 9pm and I cried all the way home. Tayla suggested turning round and going back but I was no use to him in that state. I was just too upset.

There was still a lot more to come but that was the day it really hit me. It was the day I thought that my son looked like a cancer patient. Yet he always battled on, always battled through it, even through the sepsis, losing his sight, and everything else that went on. I always worried about what was to come and always asked the nurses about it. You see on TV what treatment can do to people and you are preparing yourself for what you are going to see.

I talked to Joe Thompson about that at Christie's as Carl was being admitted, and the setbacks and complications are very tough for a mum to deal with. But you have to learn how to deal with it, otherwise you are no help. And there were some moments of relief through the whole trauma. Obviously, Maya's birth, even in those circumstances, was a special moment. We were in a hotel in Manchester after Saba had gone in to have her in Birmingham. "We need a card for Carl," I said to Tayla. "We can't leave him without a card for his baby girl." So we headed off to Sainsbury's again, and ended up near a church, with the doors open and a lady vicar standing there. I asked if we could go in and I think she could see I was distressed, and said yes. I wouldn't say I am religious – I believe what I believe – but it felt right that I should go in, sit down and say a prayer.

As we went out, I stood on the steps and the sun was shining. Tayla told me not to laugh but felt so nostalgic like someone had given her a hug and everything was going to be ok. By the time we got back to the hospital, Carl just said: "She's here." Maya had been born and it just felt like we had known from our church visit. Her arrival was the nicest thing to come out of that year, that's for sure!

It was a special moment when Saba took Maya and Mila to see Carl and he was able to meet and hold his new daughter for the first time. It was also nice for Mila to see her daddy again. I remember leaving them for a while to enjoy each other's company. I had seen the four of them together, and that was enough for me. Maya's arrival was the lift Carl needed and that we all needed. It must have been so hard for him not to be present at the birth but they were together again as a family.

Carl's football family were also so strong in how they got behind him. I remember the support from Wolves and the penalty shootout organised by Steve Plant. It was just before the first game of the season and we weren't due to see Carl, so I was feeling a bit lost. I went with Tayla to Molineux and walked into the room where it was happening. Steve's wife Andrea asked f I wanted a go and I told her who I was. She burst out crying! I had a go and scored! I stayed around a while, then headed off, knowing I would be back the next day for the game against Middlesbrough.

I had done a bit of work for that, recording a message from Carl to be played on the big screen, and it was very emotional to see that and the mosaic of 'No 1 Carl' in the stand. I always got on well with Carl and Paul on security going back through all the years I had been watching Carl and when I walked in, they always said: "Here comes Mum". They looked upset that day – I think the news had hit everyone hard – and I remember feeling so proud of Mila walking out. The fans' support was unbelievable.

I only went to two matches that season. The other was against Birmingham on the day Wolves celebrated automatic promotion. Ike had always gone to Carl's games but didn't feel strong enough that day, knowing he wouldn't be there. We went along but as they started celebrating after the game, there was one person missing. I knew that I had to leave. Emotionally, I couldn't do it. He should have been there. Wolves had just had one of their best seasons ever and he'd have loved to be involved in it. I think it was only that moment, and then Nigeria later and the World Cup, which really hit me about Carl missing out on his football.

We knew he would have to stop playing eventually, but not like that. That dream was snatched away. And yet, he is still here, we still have him, and that is so much the most important thing. The first thing that had gone through my mind when he was diagnosed with cancer was that he was going to die. It is, and probably always will be, the most horrific thing I have ever thought in my life.

It was very selfish of me, not thinking about Mila, or about Saba being heavily pregnant, but I think it was a mother's instinct. I had been a daddy's girl myself and when I lost my dad when I was 26, I wondered what the point was in living. But then Carl came running up the path, in his green coat and green and red bobble hat, and I knew he was my reason for living. That is why we have such a close bond. I poured everything into him. And so, I thought, if he was going to die, I wasn't sure how I would be able to live. But once I recovered from the shock and had that piece of paper from Manos which said they were going to cure him, that was what I held on to.

We travelled that journey with him, did what we could and he was incredibly tough and strong all the way. I remember sitting with him in the car on one of the journeys back to Manchester. He told me he didn't want anyone to ever feel sorry for him, because he didn't feel sorry for himself. I told him I didn't feel pity as such – I just wish it had never happened. I don't think he ever complained. Maybe that football mindset of getting on with it and being strong stood him in good stead. But it must have been so draining on him.

I used to look at all the treatment he was having, the chemotherapy, and didn't know how the human body could take it. It's not a nice process for a mother to watch their child go through and he seemed to suffer from every complication it was possible to experience. We knew it was never going to be plain sailing but I knew he would fight it. Everyone was there for him, his friends as well, particularly Robbie and Adam, who saw him a lot and always lifted his spirits.

It has taken its toll on everyone; obviously Carl, who had to go through it and fight it, but the rest of us as well. If there is a positive, if there is one thing that cancer has given me, it is more time with my son. It was all for the wrong reasons and it was all so horribly tough but I will always be grateful for this time I got to spend with him. We lived in each other's pockets for a lot of the 13 months of his treatment, although I did go back to work after a while.

It was such a relief when the main treatment finished and I know Carl still needs to be checked and have more treatment, but at least he is back home with Saba and the girls. And it is nice to see him putting on weight again, having come out the other side after what is such very, very harsh chemotherapy. Carl has always been very dedicated about everything he does and I know me and his Dad are both incredibly proud of him.

That's not because of his profession. Yes, it is fantastic what he achieved in his career. But we are more impressed with the young man he has become, with a lovely partner and two beautiful daughters. One thing I will always remember is telling him when we first took him up to Manchester, in that awful time not long after his diagnosis, that we were going to bring him back again at the end. And we did.

Final thoughts

By Carl's partner Saba

When I first met Carl, I was 17 and lied by saying I was 18. I was working at Selfridges part-time while at college and felt an instant attraction as I served him. I'm quite tall and thought I had found my perfect match. There was definitely a spark and we had a few dates but were young and nothing came of it.

A few years later, we started properly dating. I was in the stressful last year of my law LLB degree at Coventry Uni and working at Irwin Mitchell Solicitors part-time. We moved in together and it was very exciting to have found the love of my life and to be building a home. We had the best time and would go on lots of dates, weekend trips and holidays. He was everything I wished for and we felt perfect for each other. It was natural and easy, almost too good to be true.

Growing up, I didn't have a strong relationship with my dad and never looked up to him as a daughter should. He wasn't a bad man but couldn't show emotions properly being such a man's man and would act aggressively out of frustration. He was very strict, too. I was born in Iran and moved here at one-year-old. Mum cleaned chip shop floors while learning English. She then studied at college to become an orthodontic technician at a dental hospital, where she has now spent 20 years. She is very hard-working and the biggest idol for me and my sister.

I never thought I missed out on anything. Mum gave me everything I needed, most of all the love that is the main thing any child needs. When I turned ten, my parents separated and divorced. I remember feeling relief when I found out – I felt free. My father's behaviour and actions had created my perception of all men and I was determined to find one to not only be a respectful partner but a loving and caring father. This is exactly what I saw in Carl. Neither he nor I witnessed a loving, healthy relationship but that meant we both knew what we did not want for our future. I had already been blessed with meeting him and the love we had found was definitely worth fighting for.

My inner strength had been awoken but I didn't know what for. We had our own passions and the first thing I quickly had to learn about was football. I had never cared for it but it was a big part of his life and became a big part of mine. Carl was accustomed to a strict routine and wanted to eat certain meals in a certain order. I wanted to support him in every way I could and he would have his salmon and pasta prepared the day before a game. I slowly found our lives revolving around football and was constantly checking dates and whether games were home or away. I was nervous at every game, just hoping he would be fine. If I found out he had been injured, my heart dropped. I knew this was part of his life but it didn't ease the anxiety. Injuries could result in operations and possibly months without playing. Deep down, I knew he would always recover from physical injuries but knew that not being able to play caused him more pain than anything. He had a fair few injuries and I lost count of the times I had to help dress him or put his shoes on. I never wanted to see him defeated.

One thing he never did was bring it home. Even when his side lost or he made a mistake, it didn't impact his mood. That amazed me. I know very few people who can make that clear separation between work and home but Carl mastered it. There were also lots of highs and I was always so proud of him not just for his pure talent but his amazing worth ethic and determination to be the best he could be. He was always grounded during the peaks and, to this day, I believe this was his hidden power. He has achieved a lot and I am proud I was by his side through it all. I experienced him reaching his goals one by one.

I must admit I dreaded the random calls that would tell us he was leaving on loan. I don't like change, definitely not sudden change. I always encouraged him to go if it would mean him playing more, bring him opportunities and guide him towards his path. Although selfishly I wanted him close, I knew he was making the right decisions. We missed each other but I would drive to be with him every weekend or during the week when I had a day off uni. At some games, I revised in the players' lounge at half-time. I have fond memories of Middlesbrough in particular as he had a longer stay there and was in an apartment instead of a hotel. I am lucky to have experienced different cities through these transfers.

Other things came with football. It is easy to get carried away with the stereotypical side of it. There are a lot of egos in the game, not just players but with the wives, too. That was something Carl and me never got caught up in. He was always very humble and never the type to show off. I loved that about him. But he did enjoy going out and that was the main thing we argued about during the earlier years. He would always want to socialise with friends after games and rightly so. But that was something I found hard as I knew footballers attracted female attention. Luckily, he grew out of that stage.

Mila came along six years ago and changed our lives in ways we could never imagine. We always loved kids and couldn't wait to have our own. She was born in June, so we had the most blissful few weeks with her off-season and it felt amazing to have him home at such a special time. During the season, it seemed he was away a lot. It was hard for me being young. I was grateful we didn't have money troubles but would have preferred to have more time with him at home. Carl is the most loving, strong father and it's a joy to see him with our girls. They adore him in their lives and I feel very lucky that he will always go above and beyond for them.

He and I found we were drawn to the spiritual side and invested in powerful books that changed our outlook on life. We read The Power Of Now by Eckhart Tolle and it awakened an inner peace which has become something we try to live by. It was strange that we went through that transition together. It was as if we started to prepare for the lows that would unfold in our lives.

On the awful day we learned Carl had cancer, it just didn't feel real. It was like a bad dream and for days after, I would wake up feeling fine, then it would hit me that this was real and my whole body went numb. I constantly had a knot in my stomach. I wasn't eating and was due to give birth in six days. We were both emotional wrecks on that first day, crying in each other's arms for hours. I had never seen him vulnerable. He was always the one to reassure me as I am a bit of a worrier. Now it was my turn to reassure him.

I remember researching leukaemia online and looking at the leaflet from the hospital as we had no idea what it was. Carl preferred not to look into it and I will never forget when he looked at me and asked: "Sab, do I have a chance? Just tell me if I do or don't. That's all I want to know." My insides were crumbling as I really didn't know and the doctor told us he had a 30-40 per cent chance of being cured because of his age. But obviously I replied: "Yes, yes of course you do."

I also remember the doctor telling us Carl would be away for a month for treatment in hospital. I couldn't handle that and cried my eyes out. If they had told me then it was going to be over a year before he could be home properly, I probably would have collapsed. I thought: 'How is this even happening? The only thing that should be happening is me going into labour.' I couldn't even think about bringing a baby into that.

Once I came to some sort of acceptance, the only way I could get any sense of relief was by being productive. We did a lot of research into a plant-based diet as we had seen the positive impact it can have on your body cells and cancer cells. For a few weeks, Carl went completely vegan and was having lots of smoothies and juices. I prepared all his meals and shopped every day for organic produce. I couldn't sit down, although I was heavily pregnant.

The day Carl left for Manchester to start treatment, I was a wreck. I hid in corners to cry because I didn't want him to see me. It just felt as though the minute he walked out, that was it. I didn't know what to expect or when he was coming back. That was the start of the big change in our lives.

Carl banned me from going to Manchester as I was due to drop any day but I rang him and he sounded a bit deflated, so I called his best mates, Adam and Robbie (effectively his brothers), to drive me to see him. They were sceptical but I assured them it would be fine and urged them not to tell Carl because he would kill me. I prepared some food and Mom came over to look after Mila. In the car, I joked a few times when we were stuck in the thick of the M6 traffic that I was in labour – Adam and Robbie didn't find that very funny! Carl was very surprised and gave me a look that said: 'Why did you come?' But you could tell he was so glad we had visited.

A day or two later, I went to bed feeling our baby was going to come and she did. I accepted Carl wasn't going to be at the birth, so I wanted it done. I felt strong, although I didn't feel ready with everything going on. Any mother knows the pain of labour. It is beyond comprehensible.

I didn't want a fuss, so my friend Michelle accompanied me to hospital. The many contractions I was having at home were getting very close but were still fairly manageable. I remember thinking we should go to hospital, although I was handling the pain well. When I was admitted, we were waiting around, so I said I was in more pain than I was in order to be examined quicker.

I thought the midwife was going to say I was maybe 4cm dilated and they would send me home. But I was 7cm dilated! It was as if the emotional pain I was experiencing was greater than the physical pain. I was put straight into a water birthing pool. During the intense part of labour, I tapped out. I was having an out-of-body experience. It felt as though I was giving birth to a special baby. I felt at peace and a sense of calm entered my body. I felt everything was going to be fine. My worst dread at the time was losing Carl but those fears disappeared.

I was seeing a circle and everything was going around and back to the start. I had an enlightenment. That there is something bigger and greater than us. When Maya came, it gave us another purpose and she brought so much happiness and love to us all. The moment she was born, it all just made sense.

I couldn't get out of hospital quick enough and was discharged the same night. I just wanted to get to Manchester. I was in so much pain but was feeling the aftermath of it. I couldn't have done it without my mom, who took a week off work and helped me recover and help with Mila and Maya. I had bad uterus pain and started having mastitis from breast feeding. I remember Facetiming Carl numerous times in tears as I wasn't coping well and just wanted to go to see him. His dad, nan and everyone in the family came to see Maya and it didn't feel right that Carl wasn't with me.

As soon as I was able to sit down, I got the kids together, packed and drove to Manchester. Maya was six days old and that moment, all together in the hospital room, was the only time it really felt right. I felt whole again. From that day, I stayed in Manchester with a new-born and a four-year-old for nearly two months. We stayed in two different Airbnb's as I wanted a kitchen for preparing Carl's meals. After our intense research on nutrition, he became particular with what he ate. He was a funny eater anyway and preferred my home cooking. But it was also very important to me that he was eating nutritious foods. I just wanted him to have the best. I wanted to breast-feed Maya and give her the best, too. I wanted to give the best to everyone but myself. I would snack during the day and depended on sugary snacks for energy to get me through.

My daily routine in Manchester consisted of a visit to the Unicorn organic grocery shop. I struggled with boxes of fruit and veg to the apartment while carrying a new baby and Mila. We were in and out several times a day. No matter the weather, I would be back and forth from shopping and hospital. I had to wake up early as there was a lot I needed to cook to last Carl the whole day. He was on steroids during his first bout of treatment and that gave him an appetite, so he was enjoying his food.

I generally made were vegetable soup, chickpea or lentil curry, vegetable pie, hand-made spelt bread and pasta. Vegan meals included ample amounts of veg, herbs, grains, beans and pulses. All that chopping takes time and I stressed over not having much time to prepare properly. By lunchtime, Carl would be hungry and I would have hated him feeling frustrated from waiting too long.

It was all very strenuous. I didn't like asking for help but Mom took another week off and my friend Zara insisted on staying with me one weekend to help. It made such a difference having an extra pair of hands. I was a machine but it helped me avoid sitting there worrying about my problems.

I also knew Carl was awaiting our arrival every day and looked forward to seeing us. I couldn't wait to see him as it was the only time I could relax and enjoy some family time. I don't know how I managed. My loved ones wanted and needed me and I wanted to give them everything and wanted to be by Carl's side 24/7. I wanted to be in a little baby bubble with Maya and also to give Mila all the love and attention she needed. My circle regularly told me I needed a break and should think about myself. They were worried I would make myself ill. I never listened and luckily my body never let me down. It just kept going.

In September, Mila started reception and Carl was adamant he didn't want her life to change too much. So I would travel with the kids every weekend and every school holiday. The drive was no fun. Many parents know the pain of being stuck with a baby and curious four-year-old in the M6 roadworks. But, as a family, we were excited to go to visit Daddy and I know Carl couldn't wait either.

As soon as we arrived, we embraced each other and I felt relief just to be in his arms. Every week that had gone by, Maya and Mila were a bit older and Carl seemed to be weaker. It was hard to watch the man I adore in pain and, feeling helpless, I would just lie next to him, putting my head close to his with our foreheads touching. At that moment, I just wanted to take his pain away.

He often had no energy to interact. We were staying in a two-bed apartment and the times when he felt tired, he went to bed and I made sure the kids didn't go in. If they were too loud, I took them to Sainsbury's over the road. His appetite decreased rapidly but I made his favourite meals even if he could only manage a bite. Many times, I cried on my own, just wanting the suffering to end. I wanted him to feel normal and for us to do normal things as a family.

Carl is known for his big, strong exterior. He was the protective alpha male I always felt safe with. He protected everybody around him, even his team-mates while in goal. I know it was hard for him to lose that identity. The build-up of chemo had resulted in major weight loss, he lost his eyebrows and eyelashes and constantly looked tired and weak. He was unrecognisable to anybody who hadn't seen him for a while. But I saw him in the way I always did and was still in awe of him, even more than usual. I also felt a strong urge to protect him.

I constantly sought nurses and doctors to make sure he was alright. Carl shuddered when I did and said I was 'collaring' them by asking questions. But that's me. I needed to make sure he was in good hands. I truly believe our souls connected for a higher purpose and think we were destined to be soul mates. Life is a balance and when he was weak, I was strong. When I was down, he made me feel better by encouraging me with the right words even when he was in pain.

I will be first to admit I would definitely benefit from speaking to somebody. Carl and I have our own ways of dealing with things but I think in time we will need to speak to a professional about dealing with the trauma we have faced. I find it hard even writing this, trying to use words to do justice to what has happened to our family. I don't like talking about it and have noticed I've already suppressed some aspects as I find it hard to remember everything.

And, just when the intense chemo wasn't enough to handle, sepsis crept up on us. We were always so cautious of him catching anything but it just shows some things are unavoidable. Seeing Carl rattling from side to side with fever was a horrible picture. I was scared sitting by him giving him water and just kept praying it would pass. He could hardly talk and wasn't eating. I took a bag of food and some snacks every day and it piled up. I sat with him for hours and every day it didn't seem to change, his fever stayed frightfully high.

We didn't know then it was sepsis but knew it was bad. When the intensive care unit started examining him, it became more worrying still. Even Dr Manos, who had become a good friend, looked nervous, although he never admitted it. I would call the hospital all hours of the night and nothing changed for what felt like a lifetime. One morning, Carl was sat up in bed and I felt happier but this was cut short when he started crying. I fell to my knees. What happened? Are you ok? He told me he couldn't see the sign in front of him. My heart sank. The thought of him losing his sight was frightening but I didn't let my worry show. I consoled him and told him it was going to be okay, that this would all pass.

He was in a wheelchair when I went with him to the eye specialist. A hospital dress covered his fragile body and a mask was over his mouth. He sat with his head down and eyes full. They weren't the eyes I knew. They were defeated and sad. It was the lowest I had ever seen my man. As we walked, everyone was looking at him and I again felt protective. We waited in the lift and I stood in front of the wheelchair to cover him. To make it worse, the specialist couldn't give us a definitive answer. We were told his sight may not fully come back and, if it did, it could take weeks, months or years. Back at the room, I held him in his bed. I knew he was worried he would never see me or the kids properly again.

How much does someone have to take? He was crushed. It was then Carl felt the need to tell me that, even if his body failed him, he would never lose hope. "Saba, just know I will never give up and I will never accept death," he said. He said he constantly thought about me and the kids and we kept him pushing through. Anybody that has ever crossed paths with Carl will tell you he is the most genuine and kind-hearted man. He amazes me every day. His positive attitude throughout has been incredible. He just got on with it and never even moaned in pain.

I believe this has happened for a reason. He will go on to help others and change lives. It has brought a new taste of life for us all. We appreciate and savour even the little things like walking to the park. We have a lot to look forward to and I am grateful to have the opportunity to enjoy life with my family. Our love grew stronger from it all, we grew stronger as a team and I have come to realise it is what you call unconditional love.

My message to anybody who has to cope with cancer in the family is to stay hopeful. Even when it seems there is no hope, miracles happen. I truly believe that Carl's mentality helped him cure cancer. He had us as his driving force and support system. If you have the right mind frame, you have the best chance of beating anything. There is an end to everything and a day will come when you will feel better than today. Whatever helps you to get through it, keep doing it. Mine was being productive and giving Carl my good positive energy because I felt I was curing him in my own little way.

I am regularly asked where I found my strength and it's not something I can explain. But, on reflection, I believe it was love. Not just our love, but love of all forms. The immeasurable love shown from family members, friends and football fans gave us the right kind of energy we needed. It took a team. What happened to Carl touched many hearts and people wanted to support him in any way that they could and we will forever be grateful for that love and support.

In six years covering Wolves for the Birmingham Mail and then nine working in the club's media department, **Paul Berry** enjoyed a ringside seat as Carl Ikeme progressed from young academy prospect to established goalkeeper, for both club and country.

He was able to view almost all of the keeper's 207 Wolves appearances and work closely with him behind the scenes.

Paul also occupied the role of head of media at Wolves with overall responsibility for the club's communications at the time Carl was diagnosed with leukaemia, and for the first six months of his treatment.

With a particular interest in writing and now working as a freelance in the sporting and charity sectors, including on a part-time basis for the Cure Leukaemia charity, Paul has previously collaborated on autobiographies with Steve Bull and Dave Edwards.

He and wife Jodie have two football-loving sons, Jack and Liam, who are devoted to continuing the generational support of all things Wolves.